Armageddon:
THE FUTURE OF PLANET EARTH

BY
JIMMY
SWAGGART

Jimmy Swaggart Ministries
P.O. Box 2550
Baton Rouge, Louisiana 70821-2550

TABLE OF CONTENTS

FOREWORD

The Bible is the only book in the world that I'm aware of that tells where man came from, where man is, and where man is going.

Eschatology, the study of futuristic prophetic events according to the Bible, is one of the most interesting studies that any person could engage in. We believe the Bible is clear and replete with simple and concise directions regarding the future. It does not leave man in the dark.

To be very concise, we believe the rapture of the church (the body of Christ) could take place at any moment (I Thess. 4:16-17). We believe the rapture will be followed immediately by the great tribulation period (Matt. 24:21). The great tribulation period — lasting some seven years and known as the time of "Jacob's trouble" — will be followed by the coming of the Lord (Rev. 19:11-16). The coming of the Lord will usher in the beautiful and great millennial reign (the thousand-year reign of Christ) — (Rev. 20:3). There will be one final culminating event of wickedness that will transpire before the perfect age to come, and that is when Satan is loosed out of his prison to deceive the nations (Rev. 20:7-10). Then will come the great and beautiful perfect age without end (Rev. 21:1-27). This will be the age of victory and glory, age without end.

In outlining these events that we believe will take place in the near future, we have taken great care to write as succinctly as possible so that the reader will have little difficulty in understanding the subject at hand. There will be some repetition, because, as prophecy unfolds, different degrees of fulfillment are impacted by the same prophetic utterance.

Even though some repetition is necessary, we have elected to retain the body of thought for clarity of purpose.

Nothing in the world is more exciting than studying the blow-by-blow account of prophetic events. The world may lie in darkness not knowing what is ahead, but the faithful Bible student knows the world will not suffer destruction at the hands of a moronic dictator unleashing hydrogen and atomic destruction. He knows the world will not go out in an ice age or conversely in an overheated planet, or even die of pollution. The avid Bible student knows Jesus is coming.

I believe each chapter will unfold biblically and clearly to help you understand these great events that are transpiring and coming upon this earth. Jesus Himself said:

> *"Blessed is he that readeth, and they that hear the words of this prophecy, and keep those things which are written therein: for the time is at hand"* (Rev. 1:3).

CHAPTER 1

SODOM AND GOMORRAH

"And the Lord said, Because the cry of Sodom and Gomorrah is great, and because their sin is very grievous;

"I will go down now, and see whether they have done altogether according to the cry of it, which is come unto me; and if not, I will know.

"And the men turned their faces from thence, and went toward Sodom: but Abraham stood yet before the Lord" (Gen. 18:20-22).

"Then the Lord rained upon Sodom and upon Gomorrah brimstone and fire from the Lord out of heaven;

"And he overthrew those cities, and all the plain, and all the inhabitants of the cities, and that which grew upon the ground" (Gen. 19: 24, 25).

Masada! The word speaks of determination in almost any language and is translated "hold." In the Hebrew, both words mean the same. The Bible says, *"David . . . gat them up unto the hold"* (I Sam. 24:22).

I once stood on top of this world-famed stronghold. Naturally, my mind whirled at a hundred miles a minute as I looked out at the scene spread before me.

I gazed out over the Dead Sea. (To the north lay Jericho, one of the oldest inhabited cities on the face of the earth.) The Dead Sea is deepest toward the north end; to the south it becomes quite shallow, from three to eight feet. It is at this shallow end that most Bible scholars feel the twin cities of Sodom and Gomorrah stood. When God destroyed them, He did such a thorough job that there is no trace now left. The Dead Sea apparently covers the remains of two of the most powerful cities on the face of the earth in that day.

Bible scholars tell us that Sodom and Gomorrah probably housed some 300,000. It was, no doubt, the center of culture of the known civilized world of that day.

Then, the surrounding plains were luxuriously green and fertile, a very prosperous area, yet so wicked that the Bible records this as the only time in history that God *personally* intervened to destroy a center of population. He rained fire and brimstone on it, completely removing any physical remnant of it from the face of the earth.

At no other place in history do we have recorded where God took a personal hand in the ruination of cities. He certainly *caused* the destruction of several cities and empires through the use of agents and situations arranged and controlled by Him, but nowhere else is there a record of His *personal* intervention, as there is with Sodom and Gomorrah.

THE DESTRUCTION OF THE TWIN CITIES

The account of the fate of Sodom and Gomorrah is found in chapters 18 and 19 of Genesis. It begins with the arrival of the three men from heaven who appear before the tent of Abraham, telling him what God planned to do regarding these two cities. We know that one of these was God. The other two were no doubt angels.

Abraham was a great man in God's eyes. I'm sure he didn't rate too highly in the eyes of *men*, but to God he would one day become a great and mighty nation. All the nations of the earth would be blessed in him — through the Lord Jesus Christ.

Before God would carry out the destruction of Sodom and Gomorrah, He planned an investigation of the immediate situation:

> *"I will go down now, and see whether they*
> *have done altogether according to the cry of it,*
> *which is come unto me; and if not, I will know"*
> (Gen. 18:21).

The text then gives an account of the arrival of the two angels to Sodom that evening, to the house of Abraham's nephew, Lot. A vivid description is given of the complete corruption and evil of the men of Sodom as they surrounded Lot's house.

An undisciplined mob from every quarter raged about his house, demanding that Lot deliver the two angels to them because they were obsessed with the angels' beauty. Lot's pleas with the corrupt and evil men are a matter of record. Then we see, in Genesis 19:11, how the angel smote them with blindness, both small and great, so they could not find the door.

Their sin was grievous. God would not perform such judgment on a whim. He did what He had to for the good of the human race. What we have here is a complete parallel to the case of a surgeon cutting a cancer from a patient. The pain may be acutely piercing for the moment, but the surgery is essential if the life of the patient is to be saved.

Had no spiritual surgery been performed on Sodom and Gomorrah, the whole of civilization and the human race could have rotted away with the great evil and wickedness they represented. God performed an act of mercy. If humanity was to survive, there was no alternative.

IS IT POSSIBLE THAT THE UNITED STATES IS EVEN MORE WICKED THAN SODOM AND GOMORRAH?

Naturally, most Americans will respond by automatically rejecting this suggestion. We should, however, before we accept this conclusion, take a closer look at our situation here in America.

Jesus, speaking of some of the great miracles He had performed in the cities of Israel, made these statements:

> "Woe unto thee, Chorazin! woe unto thee, Bethsaida! for if the mighty works, which were done in you, had been done in Tyre and Sidon, they would have repented long ago in sackcloth and ashes.
>
> "But I say unto you, It shall be more tolerable for Tyre and Sidon at the day of judgment, than for you.
>
> "And thou, Capernaum, which art exalted unto heaven, shalt be brought down to hell: for if the mighty works, which have been done in thee, had been done in Sodom, it would have

remained until this day.

"But I say unto you, That it shall be more tolerable for the land of Sodom in the day of judgment, than for thee" (Matt. 11:21-24).

This statement by our Lord supplies food for thought. Sodom and Gomorrah, wicked as they were, did *not* have the light of the gospel delivered unto them as the United States has today. This nation and Canada have had more gospel preached within their borders than perhaps all the other nations of the world combined.

There are more churches in the United States and Canada than in any two comparable nations on the face of the earth; there are also more Bible schools, more Bibles printed, and more Christian literature. You can turn on your radio or television any time of the day or night and receive gospel programming. So, our national sin becomes all the more grievous in view of the light that has been given to us.

Scripture says to us:

"For unto whomsoever much is given, of him shall be much required" (Luke 12:48).

And much has been given to the twin nations of the United States and Canada. In view of the fact of all this gospel being delivered here, much is inevitably required by God. But what do we see instead? We see sin, iniquity, and blasphemy erupting like a cesspool of evil, spewing forth from the very pits of hell. Let's take a closer look at all of this.

FULFILLED IN ISRAEL SO LONG, LONG AGO

"For, behold, the Lord, the Lord of hosts, doth take away from Jerusalem and from Judah

*the stay and the staff, the whole stay of bread,
and the whole stay of water.*

*"The mighty man, and the man of war, the
judge, and the prophet, and the prudent, and the
ancient,*

*"The captain of fifty, and the honourable
man, and the counsellor, and the cunning
artificer, and the eloquent orator"* (Isa. 3:1-3).

1. NO LEADERSHIP

This Scripture recounts how, because of internal sin,
God removed from Israel the mighty men, the men of war,
the judges and the prophets, and the prudent men and the
ancients. We are seeing exactly the same thing in the
United States today. Because of this, we should pray for our
President. We should ask God to help him because the
tasks he faces are beyond the capabilities of any mortal
man. If God does *not* intervene, the United States of
America and Canada are in serious trouble. And one of the
greatest problems is — *where are the leaders?*

I stood the other day on the shell-ridden island of
Corregidor, looking at the precise spot where General
MacArthur stood. As he was forced to leave, MacArthur
promised that he would return to free the Philippine
people, *and he did just that!*

Where are the MacArthurs today? Where are the
General Pattons? When Patton was asked which way he
was going, his answer was, "There is only one direction,
and that's *forward."*

We look in vain today for the Abraham Lincolns — the
men of integrity and character who can *stand* in positions
of leadership. No nation or people can rise higher than their
leaders, and certainly we are in trouble today.

What do *we* have as leaders? Look at the Abscam scandal that revealed many of our Congressmen and Senators in all their unscrupulous greed. Bribery and corruption have become so much the order of the day that they are now almost socially acceptable. Men of integrity appear to be non-existent on the national scene.

Where are the preachers? What a far cry, today's breed, from John the Baptist who stepped out on the shores of the Jordan two thousand years ago! He said to the Pharisees and Sadducees:

> *"And now also the axe is laid unto the root of the trees: therefore every tree which bringeth not forth good fruit is hewn down, and cast into the fire"* (Matt. 3:10).

What a far cry, today's preachers, from the Jeremiahs. Paul said to the Corinthians:

> *"Woe is unto me, if I preach not the gospel"* (I Cor. 9:16).

All too often today, the public sees the preacher with lace on his sleeves, fresh from the beauty shop where he has just had his hair *styled*.

God help us — no wonder our nation is on its way to hell. We as a people have lost respect all over the world. The name "America" prompts foreigners to spit in the dirt. We've tried to *buy* our way out of our difficulties and problems; we've lowered our standards in morals in an effort not to offend the liberals and hangers-on who blaspheme God until we have become a nation of gutless and spineless pups.

Oh, there are plenty of *males* around, but not many *men!* Today, the world's picture of an "American man" is the spike-haired, dope-saturated, effeminate, nicotine-filled, lazy degenerate who, it appears, represents "the flower of America's manhood." Unfortunately, America needs *men,* not just *males.* When you don't have men, the next step is inevitable.

2. ANARCHY AND REBELLION

> *"And the people shall be oppressed, every one by another, and every one by his neighbour"* (Isa. 3:5).

We watched as Great Britain was caught up in the same sordid mess that has been soiling America for some time now. Hundreds and thousands of young men went berserk, burning down entire blocks of businesses, breaking windows, stealing whatever they wanted from the burning stores. And what was done about it? Practically nothing!

On the rare chance that someone is looking for a solution, I've got an answer to uncurbed lawlessness. In all honesty, I have *two* answers for it: the side-by-side answers of a double-barreled shotgun! I know full well that many will draw back in horror and throw up their hands in shock at Jimmy Swaggart for saying this. But the Bible says this:

> *"Because sentence against an evil work is not executed speedily, therefore the heart of the sons of men is fully set in them to do evil"* (Eccl. 8:11).

The major problem in the free world today is that *there is no punishment for crime!* In the last twenty years, in the state of California alone, for every *one* criminal that has been executed to mete out justice, *forty thousand* citizens have been executed by criminals! Just think about that *fact* for a second. This is a perfect illustration of the *mess* we're in today — all because sin is openly indulged in and, for the most part, overlooked by lawmakers.

I don't think people should be allowed to snub their noses at the police. I don't think they should be allowed to break the law with immunity. I don't think they should be allowed to rob and destroy that which *honest* men have taken years to build. I don't think people should have that right. Whatever means is required — even a double-barreled shotgun — ought to be used to stop it!

3. DISDAIN FOR AGE

"The child shall behave himself proudly against the ancient, and the base against the honourable" (Isa. 3:5b).

We have this exact situation today. The lowest, filthiest (not body-dirt filth, but "sin" filth) examples of humanity take pride in themselves and treat with disrespect those who have attained old age and positions of honor. There was a time when the elderly were loved and respected. Today, there's no respect for the elderly — or for *anybody* or *anything*. The old, the feeble, and the helpless are mugged and robbed in our major cities as if they were worn-out pieces of cheap material. Like cheap material, they are now considered good for nothing but the refuse heap after being used and abused for too many years. This is another fulfillment of the Word of God.

4. UNASHAMED SINNING

"They declare their sin as Sodom, they hide it not" (Isa. 3:9).

I saw a woman the other day being interviewed over television. She was the head of the pornography industry in Germany — her company taking in $150 million a year! She was promoted on the screen as an out-and-out celebrity! The United States, along with Germany, Sweden, and several other countries, leads the world in the publication of pornography. We're filling our land with this filth. It used to be undercover but, as the Scripture quoted earlier says, it is no longer hidden.

Marriage is scorned. How many people today are simply living together without the benefit of marriage? Fifty percent of our homes are breaking up. The other day two homosexuals had their sordid relationship "dignified" by a "marriage ceremony" performed by (would you believe?) a preacher.

Every second that goes by, twenty-four hours a day, someone attempts suicide in this nation. Do you wonder why? You turn on your television set and raw filth spews out of it. Dance programs leaving nothing to the imagination, presenting the dancers as "role models" for our young people, are piped into American homes at almost any hour of the day or night.

Long-haired, dope-crazed freaks are revered as national heroes as millions are turned-on in our drug-oriented society. It's unashamed sinning, and it's going to get worse before it gets better.

Today, we've changed the names, but we haven't changed the problems. The harlot has now become the party girl, the drunkard is an alcoholic, the sex pervert is a gay or homosexual. I'm sick to death of words like "gay" being used to amass respect for people who don't *deserve* respect. Why don't we use words descriptive of their chosen life-style — such as pervert, queer, or faggot? There are plenty of appropriate words branding these people for what they really are.

Today, the thief is a kleptomaniac, the rebel is a demonstrator, and the slothful (lazy) is the "recipient of a poverty program." Sin used to be public scandal. Now it's a mark of distinction. Teenagers brag about venereal disease. It's no longer a shame to be an unmarried mother. Marriage and purity used to be hallmarks of the United States of America, and now they're a joking matter. College boys and girls live together in the same dormitories under the guise of a "new morality." Our armed forces are riddled with "pot" and "coke" and drugs of all descriptions. God help us when the day comes that we have to defend ourselves.

5. JUVENILE DELINQUENCY

"As for my people, children are their oppressors" (Isa. 3:12).

It's obvious that history is repeating itself. The same set of circumstances that tore Israel apart years ago (because of disregard for God, His laws, and His ways) is destroying our civilization today. In many homes the *children* dictate the rules of the house and their parents meekly accept the terms they lay down. As a result of the Spocks, and others of this ilk, we've raised a generation of rebels.

The old-fashioned truths of the Bible have been cast aside. They're not needed anymore — according to the new breed of child psychologists. And what is the result of years of listening to their perverted advice? We have raised a generation of mentally disturbed children because we failed to discipline them.

All this talk about the problems facing us today because of our wayward children could probably be solved by the revival of the old-fashioned razor strap, coupled with lots of love. You see, no amount of involved philosophy contains one ounce of the wisdom of the Word of God. Solomon said in Proverbs:

> *"Train up a child in the way he should go: and when he is old, he will not depart from it"* (Prov. 22:6).

> *"Foolishness is bound in the heart of a child; but the rod of correction shall drive it far from him"* (Prov. 22:15).

> *"Withhold not correction from the child: for if thou beatest him with the rod, he shall not die.*
> *"Thou shalt beat him with the rod, and shalt deliver his soul from hell"* (Prov. 23:13, 14).

Oh, I know this is old-fashioned. Philosophers, child psychologists, and the majority of our educators and therapists will scoff at it. But despite all the renunciation, you have to admit one thing: It works, and that's more than you can say for the high-toned and far-flung theories of the "intellectuals" who *author* most of our troubles today.

6. DOMINEERING WOMEN

> *"As for my people . . . women rule over them. O my people, they which lead thee cause thee to err, and destroy the way of thy paths"* (Isa. 3:12).

I watched an interview over television some time ago. The woman being interviewed was presented as an ideal role model for all young girls. She was advocating passage of ERA. Her first marriage had broken up, ending in divorce. Then, she had taken up living with a man without the benefit of marriage and had brought her children into that environment.

Eventually, her "free love" arrangement collapsed too, and now here she was extolling the man-free life-style for all women.

I don't know all of the specifics, but this woman had problems! She made a mess of one marriage and one "shacking-up" arrangement, and now she was advocating a new ideal world of equal rights. In all honesty, I never did figure out precisely *what* she was *for*.

The *facts* are these: God made man and woman. He made man to be the head of the family. He didn't intend for him to be a dictator or a tyrant, *but He did ordain him head of the family.*

Ladies, whether you like it or not, this is God's plan. Any other order will frustrate the laws of God and will bring total destruction to those who promote such a system. Women have their role, and theirs is a position no man can adequately fill. Woman's particular and unique role was ordained by God.

I've become somewhat disturbed as I've traveled all over this nation in crusades. Quite often someone will come up to me and I can't honestly tell if it's a man or if it's a woman. It's an impossible judgment — and I'm not being sarcastic. The clothing is unisex; the hairstyle could be for either one. There's nothing there to distinguish what sex "it" is — and that is about the only way I can describe it: as "it." The individual certainly can't be described as a "he" or a "she."

Is this right? I think not. The devil has worked to get their lives so confused that the order of events laid down by God is totally unrecognizable. He has almost succeeded.

I'm concerned today that the church has often aided Satan in his effort to bring this about. How many Christian

mothers wear shorts in front of their daughters while completely disregarding the fact of their daughter's scanty
attire? This may sound old-fashioned in light of some of the
accepted fashions of today. But whether or not it *sounds*
old-fashioned, the *results* are evident all about us in the
facts of broken homes, girls pregnant in their early teens,
marriages torn to pieces, untold mental disturbances —
and all because of breaking the laws of God.

No, this is not a plea for legalism. But it is a plea for
common decency and the order laid down by God in His
Holy Word.

7. APOSTASY

> *"This know also, that in the last days
> perilous times shall come.*
> *"For men shall be lovers of their own selves,
> covetous, boasters, proud, blasphemers, dis-
> obedient to parents, unthankful, unholy,*
> *"Without natural affection, trucebreakers,
> false accusers, incontinent, fierce, despisers of
> those that are good,*
> *"Traitors, heady, highminded, lovers of
> pleasures more than lovers of God;*
> *"Having a form of godliness, but denying
> the power thereof: from such turn away"*
> (II Tim. 3:1-5).

Paul said that in the last days perilous times would
come. We're seeing this today. As I mentioned earlier in
this chapter, it won't get better, but it will get worse. The
stage is being set for the rise of the antichrist. The rapture
could take place at any moment. Above all, at this moment
in time, the child of God must do all in his power to uphold
proper Christian standards.

The only light in the world today is the Christian. Today, as never before, we need preachers — and I mean *real* preachers — called of God with a burden in their hearts that burns like flames of fire.

We need men who are men — not sissies, pipsqueaks, effeminate degenerates, or punks. The Bible says there was a *man* sent from God whose name was John. This is our crying need today. We need leaders, men who will not be swayed by money, who are not corrupt, who believe in integrity, and who will *demonstrate* this belief by their actions . . . not just their words.

Truly, men of this caliber are in short supply today. Unless we have a Holy Ghost revival, our nation will not be *defeated* by communism, but it will simply fall from the tree like a piece of rotted fruit.

MORE SINFUL THAN SODOM AND GOMORRAH

The situation today is critical. More light has been shed upon this country, more gospel preached, than at any time and place in history. Consequently, more is *expected* of us than of any other people. Yet the problems we have brought to mind barely scratch the surface.

On our telecasts lately, I have felt led of God to cry out against these problems as never before. I don't believe all of America has gone down the primrose path of loose morals and evil. God said if there were only ten righteous in Sodom and Gomorrah, He would spare the cities. He didn't find the ten, and all were destroyed.

I believe it is only the Christian segments of the populations of the United States and Canada that are saving *us* from destruction today — those who love God and who still believe in the old-fashioned standards of morality and the Bible. These are our only hope — the manifestation of Jesus Christ shining out through them.

What is the answer? The answer is *revival*. The answer is *godliness*. The answer is *righteousness*.

> *"Righteousness exalteth a nation: but sin is*
> *a reproach to any people"* (Prov. 14:34).

I think I'm preaching harder today than I've ever preached before. I'm calling a spade, a spade. I'm telling it like it is.

When God started laying it on my heart that I should do this, I didn't know what would happen. However, the mail we're receiving from people hearing the messages is heartening and encouraging. I thank God for this. America's only hope is God. Our money can't save us. Our weapons can't save us. Our intelligentsia can't save us. *Only God can save us.*

But as someone said long ago: With all the sin we see in this nation — the blasphemy against God, the absurdity of calling white black and black white, the parade of iniquity marching before our eyes — one can't help but think that if God doesn't judge America, He might have to *apologize* to Sodom and Gomorrah.

WILL THE CHURCH GO THROUGH THE GREAT TRIBULATION PERIOD?

MANY SCHOOLS OF THOUGHT

There are many and diverse opinions on the subject of whether the church of Jesus Christ will be present here on earth during the Great Tribulation or whether the church will be "raptured out" and escape it altogether. As is the case in so many areas of Bible opinion, many compelling arguments can be made for each position, and they can *all* be supported, to a greater or lesser degree, *somewhere* in Scripture.

Inasmuch as both of the *major* books concerning end-time prophecy (Daniel and Revelation) are written in symbolic language, there is even *greater* room for personal interpretation than in the more "straightforward" areas, such as the gospels and the epistles.

17

Because there *is* so much room for exposition within this area, it is important that we maintain perspective and realize that there *is* room for honest differences of opinion within the Christian community. We would do well to *listen* to the *well-thought-out* opinions of our brothers, respect them for the propriety of their opinions, and then trust in the revelations that are impressed upon our hearts by God's Holy Spirit. It is with this spirit of respect and open-mindedness that I present *my* views on the rapture and the Great Tribulation, and I hope my Christian brothers and sisters will accord the same respectful consideration to these views that I give to theirs.

Within the array of viewpoints on the issue of the rapture, some persuasions might be singled out for specific mention:

1. NON-RAPTURE

Many "modern" denominations have completely rejected any concept of the rapture. These denominations, in their repudiation of *literal* interpretation of Scripture, have completely suppressed any consideration of our Lord Jesus Christ's returning physically to reign as King of kings and Lord of lords. It is not surprising, therefore, that they also reject the idea that His church will rise to meet Him in the clouds at the *time* of His return.

2. PRE-TRIBULATIONAL RAPTURE

Those adhering to this view believe that the Lord will return to earth approximately seven years prior to His return to the Mount of Olives to assume His throne, at which time He will remove His church from the world so it will escape completely the Great Tribulation outlined in Revelation (and Daniel and other Scriptures).

3. MID-TRIBULATIONAL RAPTURE

The mid-tribulational rapturists support the position that Jesus will return for His church, but they time the event at somewhere around the *mid-point* of the seven-year Tribulation period.

4. POST-TRIBULATIONAL RAPTURE

Bible scholars of this school of thought contend that the church will remain here on earth *for* the Great Tribulation, *after which* its survivors will "rise to meet Him in the clouds" and land (along with the dead in Christ) upon the Mount of Olives where we shall *"ever be with the Lord."*

MY BELIEFS

Having outlined very briefly *some* of the various interpretations of Scriptures referring to the rapture, I want to clarify at this point that I believe in the pre-tribulational rapture. I believe the church of our Lord Jesus Christ will be *removed* from the earth at His sudden and, for the most part, unexpected appearing (like a thief in the night); that His church will be *spared* the calamitous punishments prescribed for the Great Tribulation, and will then return with Him at His Second Coming. Christ will then begin His millennial reign.

Much attention is being focused on this question, and volumes of teachings abound on all shades of opinion and all manner of viewpoints. It would seem, if *my* contacts within the Christian community are representative, that the *majority* of Christians believe the rapture will take place preceding the Great Tribulation.

There is, however, a growing supposition apparent within the Christian community which is supporting the following argument: If the church *is* going to be taken out, and you have made plans to go *through* the Great Tribulation, you will have lost nothing by preparing yourself for this eventuality. On the other hand, if the rapture *is not* to take place before the Great Tribulation and you *have not* prepared for it, you stand to lose everything. While this is certainly a logical argument, it seems to me that the Christians who accept this view are, in effect, *looking* for punishment.

It appears to me that this view harbors a feeling that the church *needs* to have God's wrath poured out upon it to purify it. I cannot support this theory. I just can't see a great and loving God pouring out His wrath upon *His own children* — children bought and adopted through the power of His Son's blood which was shed at Calvary. It doesn't make sense.

A TELLING POINT

Some time ago I heard Willard Cantelon teaching a group of students on this matter. One of those present was quite vehement in his position that the church *had* to go through the Great Tribulation. Finally, Brother Cantelon asked him this question:

"How long," he asked, "have you been a Christian?"

The young man answered that he had been a Christian for some considerable period.

"And, during all that time," Brother Cantelon persisted, "I assume you have heard many utterances in tongues, demonstrating both the gifts of tongues *and* of interpretation?"

The young man nodded in the affirmative. He nodded again when Brother Cantelon asked him whether a number of these utterances had concerned the rapture of the church.

Finally he asked the question, "Did you ever, even *one single time*, hear an utterance in tongues and the interpretation which stated that the rapture could not take place *now* or that it would be some time *before* it could take place?

"Have you ever heard a message in tongues with interpretation which suggested that the church would *not* be taken out, or that the church would be left to suffer the effects of the Great Tribulation?"

The audience sat in stunned silence. *Every* person present was searching through his or her past experiences to sift out the time when *they* might have heard such a prophetic utterance. And slowly, one by one, smiles began to light the various faces present.

"No," the young man finally said. He couldn't recall such a prophecy. He had heard many prophetic utterances and he had listened to countless messages exhorting the church to prepare itself. He had heard warnings to be ready for the time was imminent. Christ was standing at the door. His appearing could occur at any *moment*. But, he had never heard a message advising that they be prepared to wait *because it wasn't time yet!*

Search *your* memory. Surely, if you have attended services or meetings or revivals where messages and interpretations have been given, you have heard such messages referring to the end times. Have *you* ever heard a prophecy emanating from the Lord God which warned you to fortify and prepare yourself for the agony of the Great Tribulation, or for even *part* of it?

No one in the crowd before Brother Willard Cantelon that day could recall such a warning. I couldn't. In our minds the question was settled right then and there. I hope that, due to Brother Cantelon's logic, your mind has been set at rest. Nonetheless, let us search out the scriptural references to the rapture and see if we can't arrive at an answer based strictly *on* Scripture.

BIBLICAL SUPPORT FOR THE
PRE-TRIBULATIONAL RAPTURE

1. A MARKED CHANGE IN GOD'S ATTITUDE

The book of Revelation is clearly divided into *three* sections:

> *"Write the things which thou hast seen, and the things which are, and the things which shall be hereafter"* (Rev. 1:19).

Obviously, the things which John *had seen* were already in the past. These observations are found principally in the first chapter of Revelation.

The things *which are* concern, basically, the Church Age. The church existed in John's day (present tense at the time of the setting down of Revelation) and would continue until the day of the rapture (which, of course, includes this day in which we are *now* living). Chapters 2 and 3 cover this age.

The third part of Revelation concerns itself with the things which shall be *hereafter.* After what? After the rapture! Chapters 4 through 22 address themselves to the events coming *after* the rapture of the church.

Thus the book of Revelation as a whole is clearly divided into three parts. The last statement of chapter 3 says, *"He that hath an ear, let him hear what the Spirit saith [or has said] unto the churches."* This statement, in other words, *concludes* the second section (or focus) of the book of Revelation and its general coverage of prophecy referring to the Church Age.

Chapter 4 *begins* by stating, *"After this . . . ."* After what? After the Church Age!

And what *marks* the end of the Church Age? The *removal* of the church by means of the rapture. We can, therefore, conclude that everything given in Revelation after the end of chapter 3 refers to the period *after* the rapture of the church (the *end* of the Church Age).

From the time the church was inaugurated (at the moment Christ was taken up into heaven in Acts 1:9) until the time it will be raptured, we have a period of extended mercy and leniency *without* judgments from heaven. The *interim* period (between the rapture and the second advent of our Lord and Saviour), however, will be *marked* by judgments from God upon mankind.

Millions of Godly people have cried out from within their hearts for God to *stop* the forces of evil which have influenced the world for so many years. It is during the Great Tribulation period that God *will* answer these prayers and *bring* judgment to Satan's evil forces, ultimately destroying their malignant influence.

The terrible trumpets, the seals, and the judgments which shall be poured out upon the world will demonstrate the wrath and anger of God. He will show, for everyone to see, *His* response to sin, wickedness, and the filth of hell.

This will be the time when God Almighty will literally "pull off the gloves." The day of mercy will have ended.

Those left behind at the rapture will experience the Great Tribulation spoken of by Jesus. Chapters 4 and 5 of Revelation record the raptured saints (pictured symbolically as the twenty-four elders) as being with God in heaven during this period. And *with* the church safely settled in heaven, there will be no further reason for God to withhold His judgments from the earth. This will be the period described by our Lord as a time *"such as was not since the beginning of the world"* (Matt. 24:21), and it will surely be unlike any that will ever follow it.

2. THE WORDS "CHURCH" AND "CHURCHES" ARE NOT MENTIONED AGAIN.

After Revelation 3:22, the words "church" and "churches" do not again appear as referring to the church present on earth. If the church *were* to be present on earth during the Great Tribulation period, surely it would be mentioned in the Word of God after chapter 3 of Revelation. But it *isn't* mentioned.

Doesn't it seem strange, if the church of the Living God were to be present during the Great Tribulation, that God wouldn't ever have mentioned it in His Word? He speaks at great length about the church during the first three chapters. Why is the subject suddenly dropped if the church *is* to play a prominent role during this period? The answer? Of course, the church will *not* be on earth during the Great Tribulation! Rather, it will be enjoying the presence of the Lord Jesus Christ in heaven during this time.

3. THE ENTHRONED ELDERS

Most Bible students recognize the elders as representing the raptured saints and they are pictured as *only in heaven* after Revelation 4:1. They are *not* mentioned on earth and they are not referred to as *being* on earth, so it seems obvious that the reason they are *not* pictured as being on earth is because they are in heaven. That is precisely where the saints of God will *be* after the rapture has taken place.

4. RECOGNITION

Any given individual is recognized and identified by his characteristics and features. Any *body* of individuals may also be recognized by their characteristics and features. So, if the church *is* to be seen on earth during the fulfillment of the Great Tribulation period, we should be able to identify this group (as they suffer through the Tribulation) by their identifying characteristics. Search as you will, there is no such portrayal of a body of saints during this period.

On the other hand, after Revelation 4:1, the evidence of *Israel* is seen everywhere in the book of Revelation. If you will notice, Israel is not mentioned at *all* during the first three chapters. This *clarifies* that two particular groups are being dealt with in the different parts of this book.

First, the church is talked about to the time of the end of chapter 3, which marks the instant of the rapture. *After* this, the references to the church cease, and great attention is given to Israel. Reference to Israel fills the whole of Revelation in chapters 4 through 22. (The term "the elect" is also used, and some mistakenly think this refers to the church. In truth, it doesn't refer to the church at all. God uses the term "the elect" to refer to Israel.)

In actuality, the Great Tribulation period will principally involve Israel, and it will continue on through Revelation — especially from chapters 6 through 19. Focus your attention on Israel as you read these chapters.

5. THE PROMISES OF JESUS

The Master promised that some would be accounted worthy to *"escape all these things."* By "these things," He meant the calamities described in Matthew 24:4-26 and Luke 21:4-19. Those found *worthy* would stand before the Son of Man.

Who can these "worthy" ones be, other than the living saints occupying the earth just before these things come to pass? This can't refer to the 144,000 Jews in the great multitude because they are saved and raptured *after* the rapture of the church, as is proved later. If the body of

Christ remains on earth during the Great Tribulation period and goes *through* the judgments of the Great Tribulation, then what faith can we place in the words of our Saviour who promised that some would be found worthy to be taken out? Do His words not have validity or meaning?

6. II THESSALONIANS 2:6-8 OFFERS CONCLU-SIVE PROOF.

This Scripture leaves no doubt whatsoever as to *when* the rapture will take place:

> *"And now ye know what withholdeth that he might be revealed in his time.*
> *". . . only he who now letteth will let [hinder], until he be taken out of the way.*
> *"And then shall that Wicked be revealed"* (II Thes. 2:6-8).

The question here is this: What *hinders* the powers of darkness from having full sway today? What *prevents* the powers of darkness from revealing the antichrist at this time? There are *three* forces I can think of which impede the revelation of the antichrist. These are governments, the church, and the Holy Spirit. The hindrance mentioned here *has* to come from one of these sources.

Obviously, the governments of the world will not be removed from the equation because they will become even *more* prominent during the period of the Great Tribulation. (Governments will not really *hinder* the antichrist. They will, in fact, aid and abet his programs.)

The Holy Spirit will obviously not be taken out of the world during the Great Tribulation because Revelation 7:9-17 establishes that multitudes will be saved during this period. John 3:5-8, Romans 8:9, and Ephesians 2:18 attest

Armageddon:
THE FUTURE OF PLANET EARTH

BY
JIMMY
SWAGGART

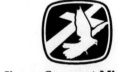

A shocking statement? On the surface perhaps. But I believe *careful* study of the Word of God will clarify, and verify, my position on this.

I believe there are four biblical conditions which will disqualify (or at least reduce the chances of) a Christian's inclusion in the great, joyous company rising to meet the Lord in the clouds. We will examine each of these conditions separately.

1. "LET US NOT SLEEP."

I Thessalonians 5:6 convinces me that "sleeping" Christians will *miss the rapture!* In Paul's letter to the church at Thessalonica, he used the Greek word *katheudo*. This means, basically, to repose one's self in sleep. But the same Greek word is used to describe the faithless, careless, indifferent virgins in Matthew 25:5. It is further used to describe the actions of the disciples who could not summon up enough dedication to watch with the Lord for one hour just before He was taken away to be crucified (Matt. 26:45). Then it is employed in Ephesians 5:14 to describe indifferent, backsliding men.

Obviously, when all the connotations of this word are studied, we can't assume that Paul was encouraging us to court insomnia, or to apply for transfer to the night shift. He was warning us to beware lest we fall back into the sinful condition from which our Lord's sacrifice saved us!

Too many Christians become indifferent with the passage of time. Living *for* Christ, *in* Christ, and *like* Christ can, after a time, become a bore. Attending church can become a bore. If we fail to work at it and fail to continually *renew* our commitment and *review* our good fortune in being where we are, it is possible to fall by the wayside.

Satan likes to remind us of the "good" things, the "exciting" things, which a Christian must shun. He tries to lead our minds back to the areas which caused us trouble *before* we were washed in the blood. And if we aren't careful, he'll *hypnotize* us, turn our eyes away from the Lord and toward those things which direct our attention to the world.

What does "hypnosis" imply? Hypnosis is a demonic sleep which subverts the *conscious* control of our minds and allows the subconscious (the deep-seated, festering things of our being) to rise to the top. Hypnosis is, in every sense of the word, a *sleep.* But it is not a natural, refreshing, *restoring* sleep; it is a disturbing, *unnatural* sleep. It is satanic, *hypnotic* sleep, I believe, which Paul is warning us against.

Just before I sat down in my office to write this chapter, I had a lengthy discussion with a young man regarding his life and commitment to God. In the course of this discussion, I described to him the *real,* day-by-day meaning of the Christian walk. Here's what I told him:

When people are first saved and begin their Christian walk, they are usually on a mountaintop high. For a time they *continue* bouncing from mountaintop to mountaintop or, as Solomon described it, *"leaping upon the mountains, skipping upon the hills"* (Sol. 2:8).

But sooner or later the season wears on and the petals fall in the rose garden until the thorns begin to show. The cherry bowl begins to display more pits than cherries. Inevitably this must happen because God *allows* it to happen.

Unfortunately, most Christians believe their Christian garden will never become invaded by weeds. They are taught by overzealous teachers and misguided preachers that a Christian walk should *never* come down from the mountaintops. But it always does. *Why* does it? Because it is only during *these* periods that we are able to stand back, evaluate our own Christian growth, and recognize the areas where we need more work!

It is our *reactions* during these periods of "valley Christianity" which determine the ultimate outcome of our Christian walk. Those Christians who are committed to Christianity only for what it will bring them, only for the "highs" it can offer, are going to be sorely tested during these spiritual "downers."

Is living for God a blessing? There just isn't any blessing in the world to compare with it. But is it an *unmixed* blessing, a daily round of ever-increasing highs? Not on your life! Every moon walk had its reentry, and every spiritual high has its return to earth. A solid, *enduring* relationship with God, an *eternal* Christian walk, can be arrived at only with hard work, sweat, and tears.

As the *public* representative of a mass ministry, you see me bounding onto platforms or entering the studio setting with a happy smile on my face. You see a man brimming over with enthusiasm and commitment to God. Perhaps we should tape a program some day when I'm *not* in that mood.

I pray every day without fail. But do you know, there are days when I don't *feel* like praying? Oh, I do it anyway. I *force* myself to pray, and once I'm into it, I'm glad I did. But there *are* those days when I just don't feel like it or I just don't feel I have the time for prayer.

I also set aside time for studying the Word of God every day. But some days things press in and I just can't see my way clear to allow that segment of the day to be used in Bible study. Matters are pressing and I need the time for other business.

Of course, on *those* days, I have to catch myself up short and have a talk with myself. What in *this* world could be more important than going before God and seeking out His wisdom as delivered through the Word? Obviously, nothing. But being *in* the world, we get caught up in the world and pretty soon start assigning undue importance to things of the world. It's as though we were *hypnotized* by matters of the world. Many times I think we actually are.

Many elements of our Christian walk become chores with the passage of time. Bible reading, right after salvation, is a great, God-given hunger. We can't get *enough* of the Word. But two years, ten years, thirty years later, after having been through the Bible twenty, thirty, or forty times, we have to *discipline* ourselves to set aside daily time to feed on the Word. Just about everything in our Christian walk is like that.

Preachers, as men chosen by God to stand and expound the things of God, don't like to point out these mundane matters. It's more fun to talk about the blessings and highs, the glory and the grandeur. But a farm would soon fall into disrepair and ruin if the chores weren't done every day. If the cows weren't milked twice a day, they'd soon stop giving milk. If they weren't fed daily and their stalls cleaned, they'd soon sicken and die. Chores keep the world turning. And if we neglect our *spiritual* chores, our *eternal* farm is going to go to wreck and ruin.

I believe we, the preachers of the Word, are at least partially to blame for the backslidden condition of many who were once saved. I think we should spend much more time preaching on the *chores* of our spiritual walks, rather than spending so much time lifting our eyes to the glories involved. We like to gather a crowd on a hill and point out the absolute beauty of the well-tended farm spread out below us. Unfortunately, we don't give equal time to the *cultivation* which produced those well-tended fields.

This is the downfall of many a Christian. They are led to believe that the Christian walk is an unrelieved blessing. Certainly, the blessings *do* come. But they are interspersed among the duties and chores of Christian commitment. A

Christian has to make a conscious *decision* to walk in the ways of God. Our human, carnal nature is such that we crave constant stimulation. But excitement and stimulation can be of the enemy. The Christian who truly wishes to be "in Christ" — to be an overcomer — must first decide whether he is willing to dedicate himself to this end every waking moment of his or her life!

We must consciously decide we're going to do the things necessary to *grow* as Christians — the distasteful things, the drab daily chores. *They're* the basis of the Christian life. And never lose sight of one fact. We *don't* do these things to "win favor" with God. No one can *earn* stature with God. Everything we have from God is through grace, His unmerited gift. *We* are the ones who need the growth aspects of the daily spiritual chores. God can get along with or without them. *We* can't!

A busy, dedicated farmer is in no danger of falling asleep as he rushes from one chore to another. And the busy, dedicated Christian is in no danger of falling asleep. It is when the farmer decides to take a break, to rest a moment under the shade of the chestnut tree, that the lulling hum of the circling bees hypnotizes him and he falls asleep.

In the same way Christians who spend time each day exercising their spiritual gifts are not prey to the devil's blandishments. But the moment they become bored, take a few days off, and pause to "refresh" themselves with an excursion into the world, they become vulnerable to his siren song and can soon fall prey to his hypnotic lures.

How many times have you been present among gatherings of "Christians" where you mention revival and no one perks up? You try to get a conversation going about some Bible passage. And then someone else brings up the Super Bowl or the latest movie. What happens? Everybody is suddenly interested. These are Christians who are *asleep* in Christ and awake to the things of the world.

What elicits responses in *your* heart? What excites you? What gets you out of your chair and heading for some activity? The true answer might come as a shock to you. It is almost as though the world has taken a spiritual sedative. We are asleep at the wheel. Church services are a bore. Living for God has become a bore. God's world just isn't as exciting as it used to be.

Or is it? Are *we* the ones who are out of step? I believe a considerable percentage of even the *Christian* segment of the world's population has been lulled to sleep by Satan's hypnotic lures. I believe when the Holy Spirit gave Paul the words in I Thessalonians, He was putting them there for Christians in *this* day. Wake up, Christian world. Sleeping Christians are *not* going to have an alarm clock just before the rapture.

2. "LET US WATCH."

Also in I Thessalonians 5:6, we are told to watch. The implication is that the Christian who does not watch is going to be overtaken by Satan. His ship is going to be capsized by the tidal wave of temptation.

Temptation is ever present. We are warned of this in Matthew 24:42-51. There are preachers who teach that we can become so immersed in goodness, so saturated with holiness, that we will never again suffer temptation. I don't believe this. I believe the child of God must be *continually* on guard. I believe Satan is committed to constantly probing for the weak spots in our spiritual armor.

A well-founded ship can survive almost *any* tempest if the helm is maintained at all times. The mightiest wave will slide under the keel if the prow of the ship meets it head-on. But if the helmsman lets his attention wander, if the ship is allowed to fall off so the wave catches it broadside, it can founder in a moment.

Constant vigilance is prescribed in this verse. If we are to complete our spiritual voyage and know the joy of being included in God's great rapture at the termination of our voyage, we must stand our watch with attention and energy. A helmsman leaning on the binnacle and drowsing the watch away between waves, is a helmsman imperiling his ship. The Christian who drowses away at his Christianity is imperiling his salvation.

All too many Christians count on God to keep them alert. They feel it is God's duty to warn them as each wave approaches. Unfortunately, it is *not* the duty of the captain to stand the wheel watch. It is the person at the helm who must maintain constant vigilance if he is to see the voyage to a successful conclusion. The helmsman who falls asleep and endangers the ship is eligible for grave disciplinary action. Christians who fail to maintain *their* vigilance can expect no better. There are consequences for our every action. Spiritual consequences are no less real than worldly ones.

This is why Paul said he died daily. The great apostle of Christ brought his body into subjection every waking day so he would not end up a castaway. And if such a magnificent man of God found it necessary to remain ever vigilant (lest he fall by the wayside), who are we to become overconfident?

Yet Christians *are* becoming smug. Their attention is wandering. Preachers and church members are becoming immersed in the world. It's a new day we're living in. The old strictures no longer count. Practices which would have been denounced a short time ago are acceptable now. Everyone else is doing it. It's a new day dawning.

But is it? Solomon said there was nothing new under the sun. Satan *knows* there's nothing new under the sun.

The modern morals and the new permissiveness are nothing new to Satan. He promoted the same things in Greece, in Rome, in Sodom and Gomorrah, and in Babylon. They're only new to us because we weren't there to see them then. And if we fall for them now, the same consequences which befell those civilizations then will befall ours.

ON AN AIRPLANE OVER THE ATLANTIC

Some time ago Frances and I were flying back to the United States from Rome, Italy. We were on a large jetliner and after we arrived at our cruising altitude, the stewardess came back along the aisle handing out earphones so we could "enjoy" the in-flight movie.

I am not blindly opposed to movies. I can see where movies *could* be a great force for good in the world, a source for leading people to God. Unfortunately, it seems obvious that the movie industry has been taken over by the enemy instead.

My family and I just don't go to movies. Perhaps by not doing so we occasionally miss out on wholesome, entertaining pictures. But I am perfectly willing to miss the occasional clean movie, because I know that in the process I miss twenty, fifty, or one hundred dirty ones. I don't even watch many movies on television. The few I've started to watch, I've turned off before they were many minutes into the story. Quite frankly, I just don't find them entertaining.

Trapped as we were on the plane, I settled back to watch this particular movie. Within a matter of minutes there were several profane remarks. I removed the earphones and was happy to see Frances and those with us do the same.

Quite frankly, I felt I was *too good* to watch that movie. Now wouldn't those who lampoon God's children make hay of *that* remark? Jimmy Swaggart is "too good" to watch movies. Yes, in my opinion, Jimmy Swaggart *is* too good to watch modern movies.

Jimmy Swaggart's mind is not a garbage can. His heart, eyes, and very being are touched by God. His body is the temple of the Holy Spirit. Jimmy Swaggart is — truly — too good to watch movies.

But even with the earphones off, there was no way to escape the large screen hanging at the front of the cabin. The scenes depicted were not of situations calculated to leave a Christian comfortable. Unhappy at being exposed to them, I rose and made my way to the little area forward by the rest rooms. Here the screen was not visible.

After a time, the stewardess approached me and asked if I felt all right. I told her I did. When she persisted and asked why I was standing there, I finally had to blurt out that it was the only place on the plane where I could escape the movie screen.

Now the sad part of this whole story is that even some Christians will smile at my "narrowness." Why? Today's *preachers* have stopped commenting on movies. They're part of the "culture" now. Christians sit through movies, watch scenes which are blatantly pornographic, laugh at jokes that are openly obscene, and then wonder why their relationship with God isn't what it used to be.

These Christians have been lulled to sleep. They've been put under a hypnotic trance by Satan because they haven't *watched*. They don't watch what they *see*, they don't watch where they *go*, and they don't watch what they *say*. And they do all this despite the fact that it is the Holy Spirit which has enjoined them *to* watch.

A BOY DYING WITH CANCER

Years ago when Frances and I were first married, my dad pastored a small church in Louisiana. Frances and I lived next door to the parsonage. I happened to be at my parents' home one afternoon when they returned from visitation.

My mother described the situation they had just left. There was a fourteen-year-old boy dying of cancer. The hospital had sent him home because there was nothing more they could do for him.

He was a grotesque sight, she said. He had cancer of the face and the malignancy had eaten away his nose. If you've ever seen a person suffering from facial cancer, you can imagine the depressing sight he presented. My mother suggested I should visit him. In fact, she said she had taken it upon herself to arrange a visit for me for Tuesday. I nodded in agreement. I could envision nothing arising to interfere with her arrangements.

Something did intervene, though. And it wasn't some outside influence. The problem that prevented the visit was heart trouble. You see, *my* heart wasn't right at the time. Satan attacked me mightily and I didn't gird my Christian armor around my loins and face him down.

In effect, I was spiritually asleep. I wasn't attending movies, I wasn't drinking (even "socially"), and I wasn't spending my evenings at nightclubs. But I *wasn't* in a proper Christian posture. I was spiritually asleep to the point where I allowed myself to wilt before the onslaught Satan directed against me. When Tuesday came, *I buckled and did what Satan wanted*. I should have faced him down and made him do what *I* wanted.

A group of young people had gathered and were ready to accompany me to the sick youth's home. Without even attempting an explanation, I told them we wouldn't be going there that evening. The following evening was the regular Wednesday service so that was out, which meant the first opportunity would be Thursday. I rescheduled the visit for Thursday afternoon.

On Thursday the young people again assembled and Frances and I drove to the boy's home. When we arrived we parked and I took my accordion and Bible from the trunk of the car. "No harm done," I thought. "Tuesday or Thursday, we *are* going to have a prayer service."

No harm done? Of course there was harm done. When we give in to even the *slightest* of Satan's leadings, we're doing harm within the kingdom of God. Even pausing to consider the enemy's promptings weakens us in our Christian resolve. But this was a matter of far more import.

There was no answer to my knock and I began to wonder if anyone was home. And then, as I began to think about leaving, the door slowly opened.

I started to introduce myself but the words froze in my throat. The puffed, defeated face of the woman standing inside the door testified to hours of weeping. She was a drained, defeated shell of a woman. Nothing but grief showed on her face. I blurted out something about coming to hold a service. I tried to mumble an apology for not keeping the appointment made by my parents.

She stood and stared at me for so long I began to wonder if she had heard me. She made no effort to open the screen door blocking our entrance. And then, as a long sigh escaped her dried lips, she made a tentative effort at opening the door.

"Come in," she said. "Come in if you'd like. You're welcome to hold a service if you care to. I'm afraid it won't do any good, though. You see, my son died last night."

What do you say at a moment like that? Her words pierced my heart like a knife. If only there were some logical reason I could find for failing to keep that appointment. To be sure, I could have come up with some *excuse* to ease her grief. The greater problem, though, was in my heart. I knew there was no excuse. I had been waylaid by the wiles of Satan and I had fallen for his deceit like the most naive, *infant* Christian. There *wasn't* any excuse. I couldn't justify my actions to her, and I certainly couldn't justify them to myself. My feeble effort at words of comfort died in my throat. I gathered up my Bible and accordion and stumbled blindly to the car.

I never met that boy. I never came to know him at all. And this was *despite* the fact that God had, within the high councils of heaven, arranged the meeting between us. God had contrived a situation where I was to be the last of God's representatives to speak to this boy on earth. And what had I done? I turned my back on God's plan, and I became the instrument to bring Satan's plan to fruition.

I don't know today whether that boy is in heaven or hell. I pray he *is* in heaven. *If* he is, he got there without any help from Jimmy Swaggart. If he is lost at this moment, I will have to stand before God someday and explain the action which allowed it to happen. What defense is there? None, absolutely none.

When I arrived home, driving the entire way without saying a word, I stumbled to the back room and fell to my knees before God.

There was nothing I could do to reverse the situation I had created. I couldn't ask God to turn back the clock as He did for Hezekiah. There is no way to remake the past. But there is *always* time to remake the future. And this was what I promised God at that time.

I would never again, as long as I lived, fail to *watch* for the snares of the enemy. Souls were in the balance. It was too late to go back and retrieve the soul of the boy who died of cancer. But there was unlimited time for saving souls in the future.

The key factor is commitment. The crucial item is dedication. If we use that lamentable and unchangeable situation as a constant reminder that it isn't just our souls, but other souls as well, which can be lost through sleep and failure to watch, perhaps some ultimate good will come out of it after all.

Failure to watch, I believe, is the second failing which can exclude a Christian from the rapture.

3. *"LET US BE SOBER."*

The antonym for sobriety is intoxication. This, of course, refers to drunkenness, but that really isn't what the Holy Spirit is discussing here.

Sobriety is tied up with walking in the light. It has to do with a never-weakening consecration to bringing about only the results God wants brought about.

Spiritual matters are *not* sources of levity. Anyone who is taking the things of God lightly is not facing facts as they are presented to God. On the other side, Satan doesn't look on his campaign as a source of mirth and amusement. He's *deadly* serious about accomplishing his ends.

Tom Landry, Christian coach of the Dallas Cowboys football team, fired a capable linebacker because he was clowning on the sidelines when the Cowboys were being badly beaten. Certainly a football game is of no great consequence in God's plan for the ages. But Coach Landry's attitude demonstrates something about Christian commitment. His attitude toward commitment, dedication, and sobriety in facing a challenge exactly parallels the point the Holy Spirit makes in I Thessalonians.

A team going into a game with a lackadaisical attitude is probably going to lose. A team with a tight-lipped, grim *determination* to win will, likely as not, end up winning! Sober resolution is a factor that *cannot* be weighed on the balance of ability, coordination, or statistics. The team soberly dedicated to taking home the victory overcomes reams of statistical reasons why they *can't* win.

Am I promoting long Christian faces then? By no means. I *am* denouncing the hail-fellow-well-met, eat-drink-and-be-merry attitude. This spells involvement with the world. But I am *not* calling for sour Christian faces.

A child of God should be the happiest person in the world. A smile should be the *badge* of a saved Christian soul. Who has more reason to smile? But a smile does not necessarily mean a light-hearted approach to a task. Consecration is an inward thing. And sober appraisal, combined with consecration, assures victory. This *should* make the Christian smile.

But the anointed words of I Thessalonians are concerned with far more than this. A sober approach to the duties of a Christian involve far more. We are in the world, but not *of* it. Although we walk *through* the world, our view should always be toward higher ground. Our only concern should lie in growing ever closer to God. We should be *developing* in the Lord. Christian golfers spend *hours* smoothing out their swings. How many are willing to devote as much time to smoothing out their spiritual attitudes?

Anything worth doing is worth practicing. Practice involves long hours devoted to *perfecting* our areas of interest. Is *anything* more important in life than seeing God's great plan brought to completion? What then is more important than practicing and perfecting our Christianity?

The Word of God tells us to be prepared at all times to give answers to anyone who would question us about this great salvation we possess. We are to study and *learn* the Word. I continually invite listeners to send for our tapes (or the tapes of other Godly men of good repute) as aids to learning the Word. Every Christian should have a good study Bible and should study the Word continuously. This is the only way to gather the answers God *enjoins* us to have.

Though the world is running around like Chicken Little crying, "The sky is falling," *Christians* should be soberly confident. Christians *know* what is going to happen while the world doesn't have the *vaguest* idea. Why is this? Because the world walks in darkness while *we* are the children of light. God has enlightened us with knowledge of *all* future events. We have no reason for doom and gloom. The earth will *not* disappear in a thermonuclear tragedy. Satan is *not* going to emerge victorious in the great conflict between enlightenment and darkness.

At any moment the trump of God will sound. Jesus Christ is coming back. The children of God who love Him with all their hearts — and live their lives for Him — will rise to meet Him in the air. The *world* will be plunged into darkness, into tribulations beyond the ability of men to describe. And then, at the culmination of all these tribulations, the Master, with all His saints, will return to defeat the antichrist, Satan, and all their earthly lieutenants. Satan will be locked away in the bottomless pit and the world will enter into the millennial reign where peace, prosperity, and justice will be the watchwords for one thousand years.

At the end of the one thousand years, Satan will be loosed for a little season, and will draw to himself those who prefer *his* brand of morality. But they will be destroyed in an instant by the brightness and glory of the Lord Jesus Christ. At this time the Lord will reconstitute the world in a flash of fire (II Pet. 3:7-13). The mighty seas will disappear. The redeemed of the earth will rule and reign (under Jesus Christ) as administrators of a new, *just* world. And the most stunning thought of all is that God Almighty will move His eternal throne from the heavenlies to planet earth.

This is our blessed hope. No, even better, it is our blessed *assurance*. God has said it, I believe it, and it's so. As children of God we should do everything within our power to live soberly, focusing our eyes on the heavenlies instead of on the world, preparing ourselves for the day when we cast off these corruptible garments.

This present world is *not* our home. We should be ready to depart it at a moment's notice. In the twinkling of an eye, at the sound of the trump, we should be ready to turn our backs on the things of the world because, as Father Abraham said, we are only pilgrims here.

Those enmeshed in the world might find their eyes averted at the moment the Lord beckons. Lot's wife looked back *after* she had been saved, and a pillar of salt is her only memorial. Christians too involved in the world should take warning from her experience. Those who fail to continue watching soberly *could* end up as tragically as Lot's wife.

The Lord could arrive at any moment. I plead with you — be in a sober state of preparedness when the trumpet sounds.

4. "PUTTING ON THE BREASTPLATE OF FAITH AND LOVE; AND FOR AN HELMET, THE HOPE OF SALVATION" (I THES. 5:8).

In other words, this Scripture directs us to become completely *covered* by God. Think of the import of that statement.

Notice that Scripture uses, by choice, a military metaphor to prescribe our posture as Christians. Why? Because we are at war! Many Christians tend to minimize this or forget it altogether. To them, the Christian walk is a side dish on the banqueting table of life. In actuality, our continuing *war* with Satan should be the centerpiece of all our waking activities.

This is a war to the death! Scripture tells us of the wages of sin — death (Rom. 6:23). The whole goal of Satan's battle in the earth is to impose death (through sin) on as many souls as possible. He has his sights trained on your soul, my soul, and the soul of every living person. Satan's only aims in life (John 10:10) are to steal, kill, and destroy. The moment we drop our guard, weaken our defenses, and relax our vigilance (in short — fail to remain sober) we become likely candidates for defeat by Satan.

There is no one in the *world* more subtle than Satan. We are warned of this in Scripture (Gen. 3:1). Subtlety implies underhandedness, deceit, and treachery. Satan does not defeat enemies by storming strongholds. *He* gains victory by tunneling away at the unsuspected weak spot in the wall.

Some time back we experienced a *tremendous* test of faith within this organization. During one particular aspect of this trial of faith, we sat discussing alternatives. During the course of the conversation, Jim Rentz studied me for a moment and said, "Brother Swaggart, we are on the front lines. We've got to *expect* this sort of thing because we aren't in the rear echelons; we're right up where the shells are exploding all around us. Our activities take place on those bridgehead areas where the enemy's firepower is *concentrated*."

As I thought about it I realized how right Jim was. And this is our *continuing* situation. And all too often Christians forget this. They think — next week or next year — *when* I get involved in a battle with Satan, I'll surely don the armor of God. Unfortunately, when we wait for the first shell to announce the attack, all too often it's too *late* to pull on the flak jacket. We're too busy diving into the foxhole.

Scripture calls it the breastplate of faith, or the *shield* of faith. In modern warfare we would no doubt refer to it as the flak jacket of faith. When we put it on and tie it firmly in place with the lacing of love, it hardly weighs an ounce. But it will protect us from the ugliest, most fearsome piece of shrapnel Satan can throw our way.

Of course, even with our *hearts* protected by a shield or jacket, we are still not invulnerable to the enemy's darts.

We still have our heads to worry about. No rational soldier or sailor would rush to man his gun without clamping on his helmet first. We, as Christians, should take an example from them.

The Word of God defines our helmet as "the hope of salvation." What does this *really* mean? It means that our awareness of the final outcome of this battle protects us against any propaganda from the enemy. We know which is to be the winning side. It's *much* easier to get through the *hard* times when you're *assured* of a seat in the convertible during the ticker tape parade. This is what God means in this Scripture. Our *heads* (minds) are protected by the blessed hope (assurance) that we win, we win, *hallelujah, we win!*

WE MUST BE ON GUARD.

Millions slouch through their Christian life believing that because they were saved *years* ago they have a ticket already printed and punched for the rapture. Lamentably, I am not convinced this is true. I don't think that if we fail to heed the explicit warnings of the Holy Spirit, we can expect to be included.

The great revelation of the rapture is given in chapter 4 of I Thessalonians. This discussion continued without interruption in chapter 5 even though the King James version breaks the chapters. Therefore, we cannot accept the discussion in chapter 4 and *ignore* the discussion in chapter 5. If we do that, we are guilty of "picking and choosing" among the Scriptures. Those who choose to run their lives on what they *like* in the Bible, while ignoring what they don't choose to follow, are treading on extremely shaky ground.

I have never noticed a passage telling us to accept what we like of God's Word and to reject what we *don't* like. I see the prudent path as one where we diligently search for God's every desire, and then *follow* these dictums to the *letter.* I believe any other course can be foolhardy at best and tragic at worst.

YEARS AGO

Some years ago Frances and I were in a midwestern state preaching a revival. This was a great church. The pastor was a great man of God. We were there for about four weeks. And one night after service was over and the congregation had drifted off, I happened to walk past the open door of the pastor's office.

I had some time before Frances was to pick me up so I paused in the office to make small talk. When I entered, though, I could see the pastor was in no mood for trivia. His head was buried in his hands and his expression was deeply troubled. I asked if there was something I could do. He shook his head sadly and said there was nothing *anyone* could do.

The previous night a brutal murder had occurred. The funeral, it turned out, was to be held in this church the next morning. Slowly the story of the murder victim began to come out.

She was a young girl of about eighteen. At one time she had attended this church. In fact, she had been *raised* in the church because her parents were deeply committed Christians. She had accepted Jesus Christ into her heart and life at an early age.

But something happened. As she grew older, she took her eyes away from the Lord and the healthy associations of the church. She began spending time with a worldly crowd which knew nothing of the Lord Jesus Christ and the things *He* stands for.

On the previous night (as the police pieced the story together), she had been out dancing with a young man. They had both been drinking. He took her home, and when he parked in front of her apartment, he began making advances. She repulsed him, and he, irrational because of the drinks, became incensed and began to strike her.

He happened to be wearing a large ring on his right hand. As he struck her repeatedly, the ring tore her face to ribbons. He beat her until she was dead — and then continued beating her for a long time *after* she was dead. The police had little trouble finding him and establishing that it was, indeed, he who had committed the crime. When they picked him up, he was almost out of his mind with remorse. He apparently could not come to terms with the fact that he had actually done it. If he could have had the chance to *undo* it, I'm sure he would have. But this didn't change the facts. She *was* dead . . . and he was a murderer in God's sight.

The pastor shook his head as he thought of having to preach the funeral sermon for this girl who had once been saved and who had died in this sordid way. She was a victim of her own desire to turn her attention to the shabby things of the world. As I slipped out of the office, he was still staring off into space and shaking his head.

The following morning I came to the church early, to pray for a time, as was my usual practice. The incident had slipped from my mind as I entered the church and made my way up to the balcony which offered a serene atmosphere in which to commune with God.

During the course of my praying, I raised my eyes and they fell on the front of the church. I was startled to see the unaccustomed sight of a casket by the altar rail. I had forgotten about the funeral, and besides, it wasn't customary to bring the casket in until just before the service. I suddenly felt led to walk downstairs and move forward to stand next to that casket.

As I stood there the words of the pastor flowed through my mind. What a tragic waste. A saved, born-again child of God, turning away from her eternal reward and casting herself into the sordid pit of the world where her only reward was to be this squalid death.

Was she saved? How can we know? Perhaps at the last moment she cried to God for help. Perhaps her last living thoughts were to cry to the Lord for mercy and forgiveness. If she *did,* I'm sure the Lord's arms enveloped her immediately. Unfortunately, I am not at all convinced this *was* what happened.

THE HOLY SPIRIT SPOKE TO ME.

The reason I question her "deathbed" salvation was because a tremendous moving of the Holy Spirit suddenly shook me. I started to weep. And this is what I believe God said to me. The words were somber, but I believe they *were* God's words and I shall never forget them.

"She used to be Mine," the words formed themselves inside my head. *"I lived with her; I strengthened her; I smoothed her path; I shepherded her. But she rejected Me.*

"She walked away the moment the world beckoned. She rejected My guidance in the things which would have strengthened her. She couldn't be bothered with the things that strengthen My children against the contrary winds. And once she wandered away from the path and entered the undergrowth, she lost her way completely. Satan overtook and the door is now eternally closed."

Lost, lost, lost. What tragedy in life could be more heartrending than this? A person who had come to know the Lord, a young woman who walked with Jesus, now irretrievably lost. And all because she allowed herself to go to *sleep* spiritually. She decided it wasn't important to *watch*. She declined to be *sober,* and decided instead to play about in the world. She neglected to *cover* herself with the armor of God. She ended up lost forever.

Dear friend, as you read this story, the Holy Spirit is speaking to your heart and telling you of the areas in your life which need to be rooted out, put under the blood, and strengthened in the Lord Jesus Christ. How do I know this? Because *none* of us is a completed project, and each of us has unfinished areas.

Time is so short. The trump of God will soon sound. Only if we utilize this time in preparing ourselves for the great day can we be *assured* of participating in the rapture. Slothful Christians are treading on quivering sands. Prudent Christians will turn their eyes *away* from the world and toward the Word. It is the Word of God that records the crucial advice given to us by the Lord Himself. In Luke 19:13, He said it all in just four words.

"Occupy," He said, *"till I come."*

CHAPTER 6

ISRAEL'S FIGHT FOR SURVIVAL

What do you call these people? Israelis? Jews? Hebrews? Zionists? Whatever the name you might prefer, a definite statement can be made: The mere mention of them will elicit a strong reaction. It might be a reaction of hatred or a reaction of love, but very seldom will it be one of indifference.

Why is it that this particular group evokes such a definite response? They are a strange and wonderful people — but in general, the world seems to wish they would just go away. Despite this, they continue on, refusing to disappear.

Who are they, or perhaps it might better be asked, *what* are they? Great empires have risen and disappeared over the years, yet this tiny and seemingly insignificant handful of people have figured more prominently in the scheme of world affairs than any single group that has ever existed.

What makes them so different? Why do they arouse such a reaction? Why is it that the majority of the world *hates* the Jews? And when we use the word "hate," we mean *hate* in its most malicious and objectionable sense.

Why did Hitler — with his Treblenka, Auschwitz, Buchenwald, and all the other camps of this type — try to exterminate an entire race? What drove him to such an extreme?

Why is it that even in the United States (the best and perhaps *only* friend Israel has) there are literally millions of Americans who harbor a deep-seated, anti-Jewish hostility? What causes this obvious animosity from otherwise "good-hearted" people?

TO KNOW THESE PEOPLE, WE SHOULD GO BACK TO THE BEGINNING.

I was seated in a restaurant, and one of my associates was sitting across the aisle with a Christian brother. I couldn't help overhearing their conversation. The brother asked my associate what nationality Abraham was, to which my associate answered instantly, "Why, he was a Jew, of course."

Before I realized what I was doing, I blurted out across the aisle, "No, he wasn't. Abraham was a Gentile."

Of course, my associate's response was not unusual. I was talking recently with a learned Bible scholar. As I pointed this out, a look of confusion crossed his face. "Of course," he said, "I never thought about that, but you're right." Most people *don't* think much about it, but Abraham was not, indeed, a Jew. Jews are, by definition, descendants of Israel (Jacob) and Jacob was Abraham's *grandson*.

After Adam and Eve fell in the Garden of Eden, plunging the world into heathenistic darkness, a terrible series of events occurred. Men turned their backs upon God, which eventually resulted in the flood of Noah's time. Then about

360 years after the flood, God spoke to Abraham — the great, great, great, great, great, great grandson of Noah.

> *"Get thee out of thy country, and from thy kindred, and from thy father's house, unto a land that I will shew thee"* (Gen. 12:1).

God further said that He would make a great nation of Abraham and bless him, and would make his name great. Then God said something to Abraham that is still in effect today:

> *"I will bless them that bless thee, and curse him that curseth thee: and in thee shall all families of the earth be blessed"* (Gen. 12:3).

This passage basically sums up all the reasons for the continuing existence of the Jewish race — and of that which has happened to them over the years. They are loved in some quarters, hated in others, but it is their unique relationship to God that has caused them to be such a "thorn in the side" for the rest of the world.

God called Abraham out of Ur of the Chaldees. This would be located in present-day Iraq, not far from the Persian Gulf. The Chaldeans were idol worshipers who worshiped, in effect, a multitude of false gods — the basic reason God told Abraham he had to leave his family and friends. The moral climate of the Chaldean society just wasn't an environment in which God could operate, even when He was dealing with one as honorable and righteous as Abraham.

Obviously, out of all the earth, God saw something special in Abraham (first called "Abram") that He saw in no other man. Abraham's "special" quality was the deep-seated desire he had in his heart for God.

There is a possibility, in the opinion of some commentators, that Abraham might well have spoken with Noah. Noah lived to the age of 950 years (350 of these were *after* the flood), so it is a definite possibility (Gen. 5:32; 7:6; 9:28, 29). There is also the possibility that Noah discussed God with Abraham and instilled in him Abraham's strong leaning toward God and righteousness. Noah was, of course, a man of deep faith. God found Noah the most righteous man of the antediluvian age.

In God's searching of the hearts of men — to find one man who could help Him carry out His will — Abraham was the man God chose. It's a numbing thought, but out of *all* the men on earth in that day, Abraham was the *only* one who could carry out the will of God.

Of course, it has been like this throughout the centuries. Jesus said later:

> *"Broad is the way, that leadeth to destruction, and many there be which go in thereat:*
> *"Because strait [narrow] is the gate, and narrow is the way, which leadeth unto life, and few there be that find it"* (Matt. 7:13, 14).

At the time of Abraham's departure from Ur of the Chaldees, God didn't tell him *where* he was going. He said instead, *"Go unto a land that I will shew thee."* The future tense implied that God *would* show him in the future, but that he would have to start the journey on faith.

Abraham, in fact, was *not* a Jew. He was a *Hebrew* — the word "Hebrew" meaning a development of *Ebereau* and Eber being Abraham's great, great grandfather (Gen. 11:16, 26). He followed God, though, as few men on earth have ever followed Him. There is the possibility that the United States of America wouldn't even be here today, and that we wouldn't know the gospel as we know it, if it hadn't been for the dedication and consecration of this man called Abraham.

It was from Abraham's loins (descendants) that the Jews came. There was Isaac, Abraham's son, and Jacob, Isaac's son. Jacob (later renamed Israel) was therefore Abraham's grandson. The nation of Israel came from the twelve sons of Israel (Jacob). *One* of Israel's sons was Judah, and it was from Judah that the nation of Judah (Judea) and the term "Jew" were derived.

When Jacob (Israel) joined his son Joseph in Egypt, there were seventy of his descendants with him. They were an insignificant number as far as the mighty Egyptian Empire was concerned, and they were basically to *remain* insignificant in number throughout history. Still, there's something remarkable about this people.

BEIRUT

I want to, for a few minutes, jump several thousand years ahead. Some time ago, along with Frances, Donnie, and certain other members of our team, I was in Beirut, Lebanon. This was during the height of the Israeli offensive to rout the PLO from Lebanese territory (Peace For Galilee).

Standing on a hill overlooking Beirut, near Israeli headcuarters, I surveyed a scene that I knew was — at least in part — fulfillment of Bible prophecy. Every few moments the ground would shake as either Israeli or PLO cannon shells exploded. Streaks of vapor in the air, left by the American-built, Israeli-flown F-16s, cut a path across the blueness of the vast Mediterranean sky. Once again, with surgical precision, the state of Israel had rolled through Lebanon and routed the PLO. Along the way they had found astronomical numbers of arms supplied to the PLO by Russia and various other communist countries.

In the city of Damour I picked up a magazine, and on the front of that magazine in Arabic was printed the words, "Our main enemy is America."

I looked at that and wondered in amazement at our misguided efforts to appease these elements that seek, with burning hatred, to destroy the United States. Yet, we seem to try to appease the evil in these people and at times have even threatened to turn our backs on Israel. God forbid that this should ever happen.

A couple of hours after standing on the hill containing the Israeli headcuarters, we were taken to the cease-fire line between the Syrians and the Israelis. I climbed the hill and looked through binoculars at Syrian soldiers a few hundred yards from where we were standing. Israeli tanks were dug in. Israeli soldiers, grimy from the heat of battle — who had been through several conflicts already — were standing with their UZI machine guns in hand. I turned to one of the soldiers and asked him this cuestion. "How do you account for the rapid pace of your advancement?"

He looked somewhat puzzled and then, with great intelligence for his age (he was about twenty-one), answered me this way: "The speed of our advance surprised us all. It was as though something went with us. It was like a power beyond our own ability."

Of course, as I stood there listening, I realized he didn't know exactly what he was talking about. Yet, what he said was extremely important. There *was* a power with them, over and above their own ability or understanding, and it was the power of God.

As I looked at the smoke and burned-out tanks, I had to ask myself, "Does God *condone* war, with all its associated bloodshed and misery? Is God in *favor* of this?"

These are not easy cuestions to answer, and it would be a tremendous oversimplification to answer with a simple yes or no. I will, however, attempt to answer them.

WHY HAS ISRAEL BEEN HATED
FOR SO LONG BY SO MANY?

1. EGYPT

Almost from the time that this people sprang from the loins of Abraham, hatred has existed, and there is a reason for it.

In the beginning, it was the nation of Egypt, with the mighty Egyptian dynasties under the pharaohs, who tried to exterminate Israel. This was during the period when Jacob's (Israel's) descendants lived in Egypt. And then, about 350 years after Israel arrived in Egypt, the pharaoh gave orders that all infant boys born to the Hebrews should be killed (Exo. 1:14-16). The Egyptian Empire, under the pharaohs, persecuted Israel terribly until God delivered them via the leadership of Moses, along with such miracles as the plagues and parting of the Red Sea.

2. THE ASSYRIAN EMPIRE

Nineveh, the capital city of Assyria at its height, was situated on the east side of the Tigris, directly across the river from the site of modern Mosul. This was the city where Jonah was sent to preach. Assyria persecuted Israel terribly at the height of their power. Nineveh, as its capital, was a large city. As described in Jonah 3:3, it *"was an exceeding great city of three days' journey."*

Sennacherib was the despot who took the northern nation of Israel into captivity about 720 B.C. The *end* of Nineveh — and the Assyrian Empire — was prophesied by two prophets: Zephaniah and Nahum. The Assyrians were a very cruel people, even to pulling the skin from their captives. Still, God showed them mercy at the time Jonah preached to them. They repented for a time and their city was spared. Eventually, though, they lapsed back into their habitual worship of idols and their other sinful practices. Assyria was in the area that is now known as Iraq (II Kings 17).

3. THE BABYLONIAN EMPIRE

This was the empire that invaded the southern state of Judah (or Judea) in 602 B.C. God allowed this invasion because of Israel's great sin. Babylon persecuted Israel terribly. It was during the captivity in Babylon that Daniel wrote the great book that bears his name. In chapter 2, where Daniel describes the great image seen by Nebuchadnezzar in a dream, Babylon is described as *"the head of gold."*

Although the empire was not physically large, it was completely totalitarian insofar as the king's authority was concerned. He was absolute in his governmental and dictatorial powers; therefore, he was pictured as *"the head of fine gold."* The Babylonian Empire, under Nebuchadnezzar, laid Israel waste, sacked the city of Jerusalem, and removed most of the Judean population to Babylon. Even though God *allowed* this to take place to punish Israel for her many sins, it was Satan's desire at the same time to run roughshod over Israel — because of the tremendous promise that the Messiah would come out of this tiny nation.

4. THE MEDO-PERSIAN EMPIRE

The Medo-Persian Empire overran the Babylonian Empire, recorded in Daniel, chapter 5. Nebuchadnezzar was dead and Belshazzar was now the king. In truth, he was the second in line from Nebuchadnezzar. King Nabonidus, his father, died in battle fighting against Cyrus, leaving the kingdom to Belshazzar.

Belshazzar was, of course, killed when the city of Babylon fell to Cyrus, as Daniel prophesied in Daniel 5:26-30. Then the great Medo-Persian Empire under Cyrus and Darius the Mede took control. Daniel himself served under these kings, just as he had under the Babylonian kings.

5. THE GRECIAN EMPIRE

The Grecian Empire was headed up by Alexander the Great, who made his empire the largest in all of recorded history — up to that time. They persecuted Israel, and God allowed it — again because of Israel's sins. Alexander the Great died about four months before his thirty-third birthday. Some say he died from syphilis, some say from drunkenness, and still others say he died of a broken heart because there were no more nations to conquer. Knowing Alexander's life-style, the first two reasons seem to be the more likely.

In any event, Alexander the Great was one of the most phenomenal military leaders who ever lived. The basic and largely unknown reason for this was that a fallen angel actually aided him in his world conquest. Of course, Alexander did not realize this himself, but Scripture reveals it to us in the words of John in Revelation 17:8. Daniel also refers to this demonic agent in Daniel 10:12, 13.

6. THE GREAT ROMAN EMPIRE

Next in succession was the mightiest empire in all of recorded history — by almost any standard that might be applied as a measuring rod. Rome ruled the world from either its eastern or western capitals for nearly fifteen hundred years. This was the empire that was ruling the known civilized world when Jesus was born in Bethlehem.

And, parenthetically, it might be mentioned that when Jesus was born, total peace was enjoyed throughout the world as a consequence of Rome's power. There was no military conflict anywhere in the world at that moment. Rome ruled supreme. Her word was law. And *because* of this, for one of the few times in history there was *truly* peace on earth at the moment the angels appeared to the shepherds, saying "*and on earth peace, good will toward men*" (Luke 2:14).

Rome ruled supreme over the tiny state of Israel, but in 70 A.D. after yet another uprising against Roman authority, Titus marched his army into Jerusalem. At that time one of the most terrifying massacres of history occurred. The temple — exactly as the Lord Jesus Christ had said would happen — was torn down, stone by stone, until no sign of it remained. A plow was run over the site to level it. Thus, one of the most beautiful buildings ever constructed was lost to mankind for all time.

Some 600,000 Jews were killed at this time. Some say there were as many as a million. But one impressive fact emerges: In all this bloodbath, not one Christian of the Early Church was lost. They remembered and acted on what the Lord Jesus Christ had said:

> "*And when ye shall see Jerusalem compassed with armies, then know that the desolation thereof is nigh.*
>
> "*Then let them which are in Judaea flee to the mountains; and let them which are in the midst of it depart out; and let not them that are in the countries enter thereinto.*
>
> "*For these be the days of vengeance, that all things which are written may be fulfilled*" (Luke 21:20-22).

The fuller meaning of this passage and the parallel passages in Mark 13 and Matthew 24 have to do with the Great Tribulation Period which is yet to come. But it had a preliminary fulfillment in 70 A.D. when Titus burned, ravaged, and sacked Jerusalem. But let's never forget, the Christians who heeded the Lord's words escaped without loss of a single life.

At that time, there were literally hundreds of thousands of Jews sold into slavery to anyone who would buy them. The price structure of the whole worldwide slave market was disrupted. While the Master had been sold for thirty pieces of silver, the price brought by individual Jews at this time was far less. And from that time on, they have suffered one persecution after another. For the last two thousand years they have been shifted, as vagabonds, from one country to another. Basically, they have been hated by all men of all nations.

7. WORLD WAR II

At the end of the conflict of 1939 to 1945, the world was appalled to hear tales of the horror of the Holocaust, as news of Hitler's gas chambers was made public. Six million Jews died as a madman tried to annihilate all of them.

All this led to a desire for a homeland of their own and was, of course, fulfillment of Bible prophecy (Isa. 11:11, 12; 14:1, 2; 27:12, 13; Jer. 22:1-8; Ezek. 11:17-20; 16:63; 20:33-44).

THE REGATHERING OF ISRAEL BEGAN IN 1948.

Against almost insurmountable odds, with 102 million Arabs opposing the formation of the state of Israel (plus

Great Britain and many other countries of the world), the tiny nation still became a reality. The Star of David, for the first time in two thousand years, flew over the sacred soil of Israel. There's still a long, long way to go before the glorious day when Israel cries, *"Behold, the Lord cometh,"* but that day *will* come — as surely as men breathe, the sun shines, and rivers flow.

Not long before President Truman died, he was asked, "What was your most important accomplishment as President of the United States?"

The President replied, with a faraway look in his eyes, "My efforts in bringing the power of the United States to bear in aiding and abetting the establishment of the nation of Israel." I would have to concur with the answer of our late President of the United States.

But now we see the combined hatred of the entire world arrayed against Israel. The Soviet Bear says she will destroy her. The might and power of Islam says she will amass six to seven million soldiers and march upon Zionist Jerusalem. The oil riches of Saudi Arabia have, by and large, gone to support the terror of the PLO in opposition to Israel.

THE UNITED STATES IS THE ONLY COUNTRY IN THE WORLD STANDING WITH ISRAEL.

C.M. Ward once said that the future of America depends upon her treatment of Israel because God said He would *"bless them that bless thee [Abram], and curse him that curseth thee"* (Gen. 12:3).

If you will look at Great Britain today, she is a shadow of what she once was. Her fortune has seemed to decline no matter what has been done or what party happens to be in power. Could this be because she opposed the formation of the state of Israel in 1948 and has continued that opposition to this day? Italy and France appear to be on the decline. Could this also be because they oppose Israel? God still honors what was said to Abraham so long ago. He will curse those who curse Israel, and He will bless those who bless her.

I firmly believe that Congress should stand behind the tiny state of Israel. This is not to say that we should condone wrongdoings, whatever they may be. But we should stand behind her with our might, our power, and the financial resources of this nation.

I believe that God will bless us abundantly for doing so. We should serve notice on the world that the arsenal of America's power stands firmly behind Israel, and that we will not tolerate any effort by any country to destroy this tiny state. I believe if we do this that God will bless and stand behind *our* country.

If in the future, because of lack of oil or anything else for that matter, we should turn our backs on the tiny state of Israel, it could mean the destruction of the United States of America. This is how strongly I feel about this, and this is how much I believe that God Almighty respects Israel.

WHY DID GOD SAY THIS TO ABRAHAM? AND WHY THE GREAT ANIMOSITY TOWARD ISRAEL?

It is because of the statement that God made to Abraham in Genesis 12:3. Here He said, *"and in thee shall all families of the earth be blessed."*

What was God referring to? What did he mean? Actually, the meaning is quite clear. God was saying that from the nation of Israel would come the Messiah — which we know to be the Lord Jesus Christ. Because of Israel and the stand she took — from the loins of Abraham to knowing the ways of God, then under the Mosaic Laws, and finally through the Messiah — Abraham and his seed would bring a blessing to the world.

In simpler terms, through Jesus Christ, the bondage of sin was broken. Through Jesus Christ (the Messiah), a blessing would come upon *all* men and no one would have to die lost; finally, *all* could be saved (Acts 16:31).

This is the reason the world hates the Jews. They don't quite understand the reason for their hatred, but the world is always in opposition to God. They always have been and always will be. Someone once said, "The world loves its own and its own loves the world."

Were you to ask the various nations of the world (or poll their individual citizens) why they hate the Jewish people (or *if* they hate the Jewish people), their answers would be varied. But whether they would realize it or not, the reason for their hatred is inspired by Satan.

Satan did everything in his power to destroy the Seed. He tried his best to kill and destroy the lineage of Christ. He hates the Jewish people because God chose them to bring the Messiah into the world. Admittedly, the Jewish people have rejected the Lord Jesus Christ as the Messiah. This is a strange irony — a strange twist of fate. The world hates the Jews because of their involvement with God Almighty and their role in bringing forth His Messiah, while at the same time the Jewish people hate the Messiah who sprang from their loins.

The *reason* the Jewish people were formulated as a race by God Almighty was for the singular purpose of bringing the Lord Jesus Christ into the world. The giving of the Mosaic Law, the advent of the prophets — these things were crucial in setting the stage for Jesus' advent. This is why God said that all families of the earth would be blessed. He was speaking of the coming of the Messiah — the Lord Jesus Christ.

I might add this: Because of Israel's following after God — even though at times they did it afar off — we must keep in mind that they were the only nation on the face of the earth that knew the true plan of God. They were the *only* people God spoke to and dealt with — simply because they were the only followers after the true God. As such, the world owes a debt of gratitude to the Jewish people. They may not understand it, but they do.

Every system of law on the face of the earth has its roots in the Mosaic Law — as given by God to Moses on Mount Sinai. It forms the foundation and basic structure of every law system in the world. The fundamentals lie in man's treatment of man, man's treatment of God, and man's worship of God.

Without such law, the world would be a jungle today. Because of it, democracy exists in many countries where it probably *wouldn't* exist if the Jewish people hadn't been around to obey and protect God's Laws.

WHAT WILL HAPPEN
TO ISRAEL IN THE FUTURE?

We have studied some of Israel's *past* involvements with God and the world. We have discussed mighty nations raised up by Satan to destroy the people of God. Even though they would sometimes come close to accomplishing this, they never *quite* succeeded because God had a plan for Israel over the ages.

If the Jews hadn't rejected God, they would have been blessed beyond measure. They would have been the leading nation on the face of the earth today. But — because they *did* rebel against God — they saw heathen nations overrun them, as allowed by God because of their sin and transgressions. And, finally — because of their rejection of Jesus Christ and their subsequent cry, *"His blood be on us, and on our children"* (Matt. 27:25) — they have known sorrow and heartache like no other people on the face of the earth have known.

Had God not had His hand upon this people, they would never have survived the forces arrayed against them. Too many nations, too many despots, too many dictators have tried to annihilate them. These individuals, inspired of hell to do away with this people, have never succeeded and never will. So let's look to the future now.

Daniel 7:7 speaks of a *re*formulation of the old Roman Empire that will return to power in the latter days. This is yet to come; it's prophetic. In the latter part of the same verse, Daniel used the term *"and it had ten horns."* This refers to the ten nations that will arise in the territory of the old Roman Empire (and which will persecute Israel dreadfully). Then it says in the eighth verse, *"there came up among them another little horn."* This, of course, will be the dreaded antichrist, who will endeavor to finally and completely destroy the people of Israel. This is recorded in Zechariah 12 through 14, and in Ezekiel 38.

Some time ago I was with one of the ambassadors from Israel and I asked him this question: "What do you see as the future of Israel?"

This was during the time of the conflict in Lebanon, and we were actually on our way to Beirut. He looked out the window for some time before answering. He had served as Israel's ambassador to various countries over the years. He was knowledgeable in the affairs of his country, but he did not know the answer to the first. "Do you know," I asked, "what *God's* plan is for Israel?" He did not know this either.

Then I said this to him, also framed as a question: "Do you realize the hour is coming when Israel, under the Messiah, will rule the entire earth?" He smiled, looked at me, and said, "Sir, I don't know about that. We're having enough problems with our little country as it is now, let alone ruling the world."

I could see he didn't understand. He was in total darkness. So let's see what the *Bible* says about it.

FIVE MAJOR EVENTS IN ISRAEL'S FUTURE

Of course, there will be *many* things that will occur, which are not foretold in the Word of God. However, these five events are major. They will affect the entire world, but the state of Israel will be particularly affected.

1. TEN NATIONS WILL BE FORMED INSIDE THE TERRITORY OF THE OLD ROMAN EMPIRE.

Israel has been a nation since 1948. Geographically she is tiny, with a population of only about four million. There are any number of *cities* in the world with more people. Still, she exerts an influence on world affairs far beyond her actual size. There are good reasons for this.

First of all, she is no doubt the only *real* friend the United States has in this part of the world.

Second, Israel is the land bridge between Africa, Europe, and Asia.

Third, even though Israel produces little or no oil, she is surrounded by the greatest oil-producing nations in the world (Saudi Arabia, Iraq, Iran, Libya, etc.). This creates a problem. While the United States would like to maintain close ties and friendly relations with her oil suppliers, the fact is, Israel is the only nation in this area that we can really trust. If it were not for Israel, only God knows what would happen to our influence there. She has a great stabilizing effect on the whole Middle East. Even the nations that detest her (such as Saudi Arabia, Iran, etc.) depend on her for much more than is generally known.

In Israel's quest for her traditional boundaries, the West Bank has become the focal point of much controversy. President Reagan has made peace proposals that would involve Israel's giving up the West Bank to Jordan and the PLO, maintaining only token controls. This is, of course, unthinkable.

I predict that in the not-too-distant future, Israel will totally annex the West Bank. This must come about. The West Bank is just too much Israel. It is as much an inherent part of Israel as any other area of the country. So the West Bank will soon be annexed. There will be much discussion when this takes place — by the PLO, Egypt, and others — but little will ultimately be done about it.

Little by little, Jerusalem will come to be accepted as the capital of Israel. Of course, Tel Aviv is currently the nominal capital of this tiny country, but this is only because the Palestinians claim a large part of Jerusalem. However, Jerusalem will not be given up to anyone else. It is totally controlled by the Jewish people and, as one Israeli officer recently told me, "Jerusalem is our capital — not Tel Aviv." He is certainly correct, and all nations of the world will eventually come to accept Jerusalem in this vein.

Actually, according to the Word of God, the nation of Israel is going to become more and more powerful. There will no doubt be skirmishes, probably even wars, but she will not be defeated in the foreseeable future.

Daniel spoke of the great Roman Empire that was to arise several hundred years after his death (Dan. 7:7). In the latter portion of verse 7, he stated *"and it had ten horns."* Then in the first part of verse 8 he said, *"I considered the horns."* Then he says, in verse 24, *"And the ten horns out of this kingdom are ten kings that shall arise."*

Bible students recognize this as ten nations that will be formed out of the old Roman Empire territory. Whether these ten nations will totally replace the twenty-five or so nations now occupying this area, or whether they will just replace some of them, is not known. But most Bible scholars believe that a great war is going to be fought in order for these ten "horns" to become the ten nations that will fulfill Bible prophecy. It does use the phrase *"out of this kingdom,"* so we can be certain of the area from which it will spring. More than likely they will surround Israel. We know that four of these nations will be Turkey, Syria, Greece, and Egypt. The identity of the other six is not stated.

During this time of confusion there is no scriptural indication of the destruction of Israel. There will be much conflict among the other nations, and while these influences will no doubt *touch* Israel, she will be in no great danger during this time. We can conclude this from that which immediately follows:

2. THE ANTICHRIST WILL MAKE A SEVEN-YEAR NONAGGRESSION PACT WITH ISRAEL.

> *"And another [meaning the antichrist] shall be diverse from the first, and he shall subdue three kings."* (Dan. 7:24).

The three kings spoken of here are Greece, Turkey, and Egypt. Of course, we know that the antichrist will come from Syria. Ancient Syria covered the territories of present-day Lebanon, Iraq, Iran, and Syria — so the antichrist could actually come from any of these countries and still fulfill Bible prophecy. He will probably be a Syrian Jew, because at this time Israel will be a powerful nation. Actually, she is powerful right now. Someone made the statement, during the Lebanese conflict, that Israel was the third-most-powerful nation in the world — following only the United States and the Soviet Union. Whether this would hold true in regard to such countries as Great Britain in an extended conflict is not really known, however.

When the antichrist makes his debut, the Bible says he will be tremendously powerful.

> *"And his power shall be mighty. . . and he shall destroy wonderfully, and shall prosper, and practise, and shall destroy the mighty and the holy people [Israel]"* (Dan. 8:24).

However, in the beginning Israel will think the antichrist is the "Messiah." This is what the Master meant when He made this statement:

> *"Ye receive me not: [but] if another shall come in his own name, him ye will receive"* (John 5:43).

The "another" spoken of here is the antichrist, and this is exactly what will happen. The Jewish people rejected the true Messiah but they will accept the false one as the ultimate solution to all their problems.

Many false Messiahs have arisen in Israel since the first Messianic prophecies were given back in the days of Abraham, Isaac, and Jacob. And Israel realizes today that her only real hope lies in the coming of the Messiah. They are somewhat divided as to how this will come about and just who it will be, but the antichrist will no doubt extend friendly overtures toward Israel and will *in all likelihood* be Jewish. In all probability, these overtures of peace and friendship will convince the Israelis he is the true Messiah.

Something else must also occur in Israel, but only God knows how it will happen. We know that the Jewish temple will be rebuilt. Of course, the Jewish people haven't had a temple since 70 A.D. Titus destroyed the beautiful temple built by Herod more than 1900 years ago.

The temple is the focal point of Jewish worship, and here, in the rebuilt temple, they will reinstitute the old Jewish blood sacrifices. At the present time, the sacred and hallowed ground of the temple is occupied by the Dome of the Rock, a sacred Islamic holy place. Naturally, this is an abomination to Israel.

There's been little they could do, however, because its removal would cause a catastrophic war with the tens of millions of Moslems throughout the world. The Moslems revere the Dome of the Rock almost as much as Mecca. It may be that the antichrist will play an important role in neutralizing this area, making it possible for Israel to rebuild the temple. The Bible is mute on this point, but we do know that great successes will help the antichrist to gain favor with the Jewish people. This could be the basis for Israel's willingness to sign his treaty and to accept him as the Messiah. We are told this in Daniel 9:27, where it says, *"And he [the antichrist] shall confirm the covenant with many for one week."* And, of course, we know that this "week" means *a week of years* — actually constituting seven years.

Israel will believe at this point that she has solved all her problems. She will now have the protection of the antichrist, who she conceivably accepts as the Messiah, no longer fearing the other countries of the world. From this point on it would appear that nothing could stop her. However, something else is about to happen.

3. THE ANTICHRIST WILL BREAK THIS NON-AGGRESSION PACT WITH ISRAEL AFTER THREE AND ONE-HALF YEARS.

We are told in Daniel 9:27, that *"in the midst of the week [after three and one-half years] he shall cause the sacrifice and the oblation to cease."* We know from this that Israel will have reinstated the ritual sacrifices and that the antichrist will have begun his short-lived but extremely cruel oppression of Israel. He will actually declare war on her. This is the next great conflict spoken of in the Bible concerning Israel.

There may be any number of events occurring between now and then, but this is the only one foretold in the Bible. His forces will totally dominate Israel, and this will be the first time in modern history that they are invaded and defeated.

There will be tremendous exultation throughout the world because at long last it will appear that the Palestinians, Islam, perhaps the Soviet Union, and others will realize their desires. Israel will be defeated and Zionism destroyed. The antichrist will conquer Israel and make the new Jewish temple his capital (Dan. 7:21-25; 8:9-14, 22-25; II Thes. 2:3, 4; Rev. 13:1-18; 17:8-17). He will erect a statue of himself in the temple, in the Holy of Holies, and will thus pollute and desecrate it, creating the abomination of desolation (Dan. 8:9-14; 9:27; 11:45; II Thess. 2:3, 4; Rev. 13:1-18).

It will be the intention of the antichrist to completely destroy Israel. However, God will intervene. As a remnant from Jerusalem and other cities in Israel attempt escape, the antichrist's armies will pursue with the goal of complete annihilation. Here, however, God will supernaturally cause the ground to open up and swallow the armies of the antichrist (dragon) as they pursue the Israel remnant's flight into Moab and Edom (Dan. 11:41; Isa. 16:1-5; Matt. 24:16; Rev. 12:14-17). It will, no doubt, be viewed by the world as an "earthquake." This will cause the antichrist to abandon for the moment this remnant fleeing toward the area known as Petra.

After this, his evil intentions can easily be carried out, but he will be diverted, as Daniel tells us:

> *"Tidings out of the east and out of the north shall trouble him: therefore he shall go forth with great fury"* (Dan. 11:44).

We don't know *precisely* what these "tidings" will be, but they will, no doubt, constitute a threat against the antichrist. He will, therefore, set out to conquer these areas which will probably constitute Germany and Russia to the north and China to the east. Undoubtedly, other countries will also be involved. This war between the antichrist and the countries to the north and east will cause Israel's persecution to be shortened. We are told this in Matthew 24:22.

While the antichrist's attention is occupied with this world conflict, many Jewish people will again filter back to the land of Israel. It would seem, from the biblical descriptions, that by and large the antichrist's domination of Israel will now be lifted. She will once again be master of her own country.

4. THE ANTICHRIST WILL COME DOWN IN FURY TO DESTROY COMPLETELY THE NATION OF ISRAEL. THIS IS TO BE THE "FINAL SOLUTION."

Ezekiel 38 tells us of this. Many people assume this is the Soviet Union, but it is actually the antichrist. He will probably go under the title of Gog. Ezekiel 38 and 39 graphically describe this. The antichrist will once and for all, with diabolical fury, hurl himself against Israel, covering the land. Many nations will be with him, and it will be his intention to finally annihilate the Jewish people. But, as the Bible tells us:

> *"Then shall the Lord go forth, and fight against those nations, as when he fought in the day of battle"* (Zech. 14:3).

Actually, part of the city of Jerusalem will be taken by the antichrist again, repeating his earlier victory there. This will take place at the end of the Great Tribulation Period — just before the Second Coming of Christ. The Bible says the houses will be robbed, the women ravished, and half the city will fall. But, suddenly, Christ will make His appearance with *His* armies and defeat the antichrist in a tremendous one-day battle: the Battle of Armageddon. This is the culmination of the antichrist's plan to destroy Israel, conquer God Almighty, and gain control of the world. He does not succeed.

The Lord will personally defend the inhabitants of Jerusalem as they are about to be destroyed (Zech. 12:8-14; 14:1-5). He will help and protect earthly Israel, making her invincible in battle. Israel will also receive the assistance of the heavenly army of angels and saints, led by Jesus Christ personally (Isa. 63:1-6; Joel 2:11; II Thes. 1:7-10; Jude 14, 15; Rev. 19:11-21).

5. ISRAEL'S FUTURE WILL CLIMAX (OR REALLY BEGIN) WITH JESUS CHRIST FINALLY BEING ACCEPTED AS THEIR MESSIAH, AND WITH THEM SPREADING HIS GOSPEL THROUGHOUT THE WORLD.

The Lord said that after the Battle of Armageddon He would have mercy on the *whole house of Israel* and they would dwell safely in their own land. None will make them afraid, and they will be brought back from all the nations of their dispersal (Ezek. 39:26, 27). God said He would not hide His face from them anymore, for He will have redeemed them and poured out His Spirit upon them (Ezek. 39:28, 29).

In Isaiah 66:19, 20 we are told that the Lord will send Jewish missionaries throughout the world to spread the word of His fame and glory. He speaks also of the Jews who are to be priests and Levites once again in the millennial temple. He then promises that in the *"new heavens"* and the *"new earth"* (Isa. 66:22) that Israel's seed and name will remain before Him forever and forever.

After the Battle of Armageddon we are told that *"the wealth of all the heathen round about shall be gathered"* (Zech. 14:14) and divided in the midst of Judah. Of course, this does not mean *every* nation of the earth, but rather the nations that accompanied the antichrist against Israel.

We are also told in Zechariah 14:16 that these same nations will go up to Jerusalem from year to year to worship the King, the Lord of hosts, and to keep the Feast of Tabernacles.

The ultimate future of Israel is this:

> *"In that day there shall be a fountain opened to the house of David and to the inhabitants of Jerusalem for sin and for uncleanness.*
>
> *"And it shall come to pass in that day, saith the Lord of hosts, that I will cut off the names of the idols out of the land, and they shall no more be remembered: and also I will cause the prophets and the unclean spirit to pass out of the land"* (Zech. 13:1, 2).

CHAPTER 7

WHEN GOD FIGHTS RUSSIA

"And the word of the Lord came unto me, saying,

"Son of man, set thy face against Gog, the land of Magog, the chief prince of Meshech and Tubal, and prophesy against him,

"And say, Thus saith the Lord God; Behold, I am against thee, O Gog, the chief prince of Meshech and Tubal:

"And I will turn thee back, and put hooks into thy jaws, and I will bring thee forth, and all thine army, horses and horsemen, all of them clothed with all sorts of armour, even a great company with bucklers and shields, all of them handling swords" (Ezek. 38:1-4).

Ezekiel 38 is one of the most commonly quoted scriptural passages, especially among evangelists, pastors, and Bible teachers who have a particular interest in Bible prophecy. It is almost universally considered to be the description of an invasion of Israel by the Soviet Union. Clearly, it would appear that the land of Israel *will* be invaded. The question remains, however, is it the Soviet Union that will do the invading? Is there clear inference that it is Russia that is spoken of in Ezekiel 38 — or is this just one of those "facts" that is taken for granted?

And if Russia is not "Gog" of Ezekiel 38 and 39, what *is* to become of Russia in the last days? Clearly, as one of the two great world powers, she will not simply "dwindle away" in the short time remaining before the Lord's return. And what of Israel? What of *her* future? And, finally, what of the United States? It is clear from this chapter in Ezekiel (and other Scriptures) that a great end-time battle will be fought just prior to the return of Jesus Christ to institute His righteous millennial reign. What will be the role of the United States in this great battle?

The Bible has a great deal to say about this great last-day confrontation, but — as with most Bible prophecies — there are great gaps left between the hard facts presented. The facts we do have, however, can be assembled to rough out the general picture of this time.

I hope, throughout this chapter, to demonstrate these three points as revealed in Scripture:

1. A world conflict is coming that will greatly change the map of the world. It *will* involve the Soviet Union.

2. There is no actual indication in the Word of God that Israel will be invaded by *Russia*. Ezekiel has little reference to the Soviet Union and is actually a prophecy of an *amalgamation* (a merging) of nations (*including* the Soviet Union) which will invade Israel.

3. Of all the invasions of Israel in modern times, this will come closest to destroying her. It will not succeed, however.

THE SOVIET UNION AND COMMUNISM

Communism is the worst form of government ever conceived by the mind of hell. I am firmly convinced it is diabolical in concept, Satan's ultimate political tool, and it shouldn't really be dignified by the term "government." It is, rather, little more than institutionalized slavery.

The Soviet Union is, of course, the prototype of a communist nation. Communism had its first trial in Russia — starting in 1917 — after being a theoretical concept for many years. Today — after seventy years to demonstrate its virtues, and after export to a major portion of the globe — communism has proven only that it is unworkable in practice.

There isn't a communist government under the sun that would last out the day if its people were allowed to vote. As was demonstrated in Poland, brute force is used to keep the masses under the yoke. Whether they were aware of it or not, Marx, Lenin, and Trotsky were actually the pawns of Satan as they conspired to impose their atheistic philosophy on the unfortunate people of Russia. Everything about communism is opposed to Godly principles — brute force, slavery, right by might, and no semblance of free choice except among the small, ruling elite.

Still, this misbegotten principle — promoted by the devil and abetted by any number of misguided allies — has managed to become the greatest tool for enslavement and suppression of human rights in history. Today more people live under communism than the *total* populations ground under the heels of Rome, Alexander, Nebuchadnezzar, and all the despots of history.

Under communism, a self-designated "elite" (actually the most ruthless and bloodthirsty survivors of the early plotters) takes what it wants by force. It has no regard for humanity, no concern for the most basic of human principles. It concerns itself only with the end result — what do *I* want? Communism will go to any lengths — the torture of hordes of people, mass murder — to realize its ends. Consequently, more people have been killed to advance the cause of communism than any other ideology in all of history.

It is totally materialistic in concept. Its god is force; its goal is power. By using totalitarian force and exerting total control over its people, it has managed to build one of the greatest armies on the face of the earth.

The Soviet Union is the center of infection for world communism, and it is from this draining sore that the contagion of communism has spread throughout much of the world. But despite the size of its Army, Navy, and Air Force, the Soviet Union is in fact little more than a third-world country. Actually, some third-world countries have a higher standard of living than the Soviet Union. Its people are backward, and instead of the state serving the people, the people are slaves to the state.

Whenever newsreel footage or television tape of Russia is shown in the United States or Canada, or when misguided apologists appear in Russia to extol its virtues, they invariably focus on a few prime locations that project a sense of prosperity. In fact, signs of prosperity are few and far between. Most things taken for granted in the United States (labor-saving devices, conveniences, and technical advances that make life easier) are all but unknown in the Soviet Union.

This largest country on the face of the earth can't feed its own population and must import hundreds of millions of dollars worth of grain from the United States and other countries annually. This isn't because they lack soil, favorable growing conditions, or labor. It is a total consequence of the inherent evils of communism.

Communism destroys all incentive. The laborer is *not* considered worthy of his hire, competence is not admired, and ambition is discouraged. The basic premise is that the great gray mass should produce for the chosen few — who reap the rewards of everyone's labor. Of course, once it becomes evident that excellence is *not* rewarded, no one tries to excel. Soon the only competition is to see who can do the *least,* and finally there is great motion with little actual production. Ultimately, it is an unworkable system.

COMMUNISM'S LEADERS

When the United States sits down at the bargaining table and proposes to deal with the leaders of the Soviet Union (or their subordinates), they are not dealing with responsible governmental leaders. They are presenting themselves to little more than thugs, gangsters, and hoodlums. Actually, the average American Mafia chieftain could be considered fainthearted by comparison. These are men who have gained their positions by being more ruthless, more brutal, and more bloodthirsty than their contemporaries.

In other words, they climbed to their positions over the dead bodies of hundreds (and sometimes thousands or even millions) of their fellow citizens. They are sadists and pathological liars and have openly declared, time and time again, that they have no intention of abiding by any treaty they make. Still, the United States naively signs treaty after treaty — despite a history of broken agreements in the past.

We seem incapable of learning from past confrontations with the Soviets. It may well be said, at some time in the future, that no nation has ever been so grievously deceived, duped, and taken in as the United States has in its dealings with the Soviet Union.

Realistically, since the Russian leaders have *no* intention of observing them, the United States should not sign *any* agreements with Russia. They use agreements only to further their own purposes. Whether these agreements are in the areas of technology, science, the military, or finance — they serve only the communistic purpose. Otherwise they wouldn't be signed. We keep our treaties religiously; they do not. Because of such tactics, Russia becomes stronger and stronger while we become weaker and weaker.

The fundamental Christian basis of this country — eroded though it may be today — still promotes a sense of fair play. We believe in "play by the rules" and "give the other guy an even break." It's like a sporting contest where one side adheres to the rules while their opponents use every foul tactic available. While in a sporting event this would lead only to a black mark in the loss column, here we are dealing with life and death.

It may well be said at some time in the future that never has so much been given up for so little in return. Such is the result of considering communist dictators as men of integrity.

THE UNITED STATES' FINANCIAL PICTURE

The United States is experiencing problems with giant banks such as Chase Manhattan, Manufacturer's Hanover, and Chemical Bank of New York. Why? Because they have loaned many billions of dollars to third-world countries — many of them behind the Iron Curtain. One defector from Poland stated that when these large sums were offered to Poland, some cautioned, "There's no possible way we can pay this back." The Polish leaders archly replied, "What difference does that make? We don't *intend* to pay it back." The attitude was, "Let the capitalist bankers worry about it; we aren't worried."

And what does all this mean to the average man on the street here in America? Only that if the large financial institutions are threatened with bankruptcy — they will not be allowed to suffer the consequences of their greed and incompetence. They will be "bailed out" by a system called "monetarization" of the debt. And what does "monetarization" mean? It means that these foreign debts will be paid back to the big bankers so they don't lose a cent — *but by the American taxpayers!* The money-lords won't suffer for their greed — you and I will! The dollars Poland, Bulgaria, Romania, and others owe could be added to the deficit that already threatens to bankrupt the United States.

Oh, the tragedy of it! It could well be said that we, the average American citizens, in some ways have financed Russia's invasion and oppression of Afghanistan. We have paid for the nuclear warheads that now threaten us from Cuba. We have paid for the ships that will put American sailors under the sea at the first hint of trouble in the Mediterranean.

Actually, it was American dollars, by way of loans passing through satellite nations, that have helped finance Russia's support of terrorism and subversion throughout the world. How reassuring it is to know that America's diplomacy, politics, and finances are in such capable hands.

If it weren't for American know-how, technology, and money, communism would have fallen of internal rot long ago. But because of our gullibility and our gross stupidity in supporting the Soviet Union financially — at interest rates far lower than those paid by American citizens— they have continued to be a disrupting force in world society.

It is a waste of time to indulge in any type of SALT or START talks — or any other type of negotiation — with these subhumans. If we were rational, we would withdraw our diplomats from the Soviet Union and order the United

Nations to leave this country. The only thing preventing Russia from completing her plan for world domination now is Almighty God and the military might of the United States. God help us if we ever allow ourselves to be weakened to the point where the Soviet Union is no longer afraid of our power. If we do, that is the day the United States will cease to exist and the world will fall into a new Dark Age.

SURVIVAL BY FORCE

Communism, due to its nature and internal structure, can only survive by expansion *and conquest*. Russia's desire to dominate the Persian Gulf — which contains the greatest reserves of oil in the world — is a long-standing and well-documented fact. It has been correctly stated that "he who rules Mideast oil rules the world."

Russia's effort to control this area has been by proxy thus far. Egypt was the first surrogate — until Russia's ever-more-strident demands caused Sadat to expel them. Since then Libya, Iraq, Syria, Lebanon, and the PLO have all, at one time or another, received massive infusions of Soviet military supplies. In 1981 alone, the Soviet Union sold third-world countries in the Persian Gulf nearly $14 billion in arms. The Arab states accounted for nearly ninety percent of these sales.

During Israel's raid into Lebanon to rout the PLO, some 500 Soviet tanks were lost, and billions of dollars worth of Soviet equipment (including some 90 MIGs, 144 armored vehicles, 359 sophisticated communication devices, and 515 heavy artillery pieces) were destroyed or captured. Military authorities estimated that more than 150 ten-ton Mack trucks — manned by one thousand soldiers — would be required for six weeks to haul all this equipment back to Israel. The Soviet Union had twenty Russian divisions in central Asia, bordering Afghanistan and Iran, and a rapid redeployment force of some thirty divisions. Soviet influence is rapidly growing in Iran, and experts state that Iran will become a Soviet satellite on the death of Khomeini.

Twelve Soviet divisions ring the Turkish border near the Black Sea, and the Soviets have over 100 thousand troops in Afghanistan. There are eleven Russian warships and fifteen supply ships in the Arabian Gulf. This tremendous Russian arms buildup can't possibly be construed as defensive in nature. Its clear purpose is to rule the world — and the prime enemy is the United States.

I stood in the ruins of Damour, Lebanon, in July of 1982, immediately after Israel's incursion into that country and chanced to pick up a magazine lying on the ground. One of the men with us who understood Arabic translated the words printed at the bottom of the cover page. It said, "Our chief enemy is America."

Israel is the only country in the Middle East that stands as a hindrance to the Russian Bear's communization of the oil-rich Persian Gulf. Sixty percent of the world's oil flows from this area.

General David C. Jones stated that direct intervention by the Soviets (or their proxies) has the potential to bring the industrial west to its knees without a single Soviet soldier having to cross a western border. This is *the* hot spot of the world, and this is the area where age-old prophecies focus.

A GIGANTIC CONFLICT THAT COULD CHANGE THE BOUNDARIES OF NATIONS

Strangely enough, despite all the preparations made by the Russian Bear and all the ominous statistics we have given, there is no indication in the Bible that the Soviet Union will invade the Middle East. It could happen, and the Bible doesn't say it *won't* happen. It is merely silent on the question of Russia's precise role.

Despite all the totalitarian efforts by communist dictators and despite their huge arms buildup, communism is actually coming apart at the seams. The average living conditions in Russia are deplorable. Up until now they have had a barely acceptable living standard. Now, however, due to world economic conditions, the situation in the Soviet Union and in client states is steadily deteriorating. There is a very real possibility of a famine that could claim millions of Soviet citizens. They can't feed themselves because their social system discourages production — as the food supply situation in Poland has demonstrated. Their formerly large supplies of gold are being depleted to pay for wheat and other staples from the west. While they are not currently at the point of disintegration, they are certainly *headed* in that direction.

The Soviet Union has another problem. It is a mixture of many nationalities and races — many of whom hate their Russian masters and communism in any form. They can't be trusted nor depended upon to follow the communist line. And these other races are breeding faster than the Russians in an ever-constricting minority. To be sure, the police-state system makes collapse unlikely in the near future, but at the same time there has been a definite weakening of Russia's monolithic structure.

THE TEN HORNS

The Bible doesn't go into detail to mention such matters, but it does say this in Daniel:

> *"After this I saw in the night visions, and behold a fourth beast, dreadful and terrible, and strong exceedingly; and it had great iron teeth:*

it devoured and brake in pieces, and stamped the
residue with the feet of it: and it was diverse from
all the beasts that were before it; and it had ten
horns" (Dan. 7:7).

We want to concentrate here on the ten horns. Daniel
went on to say:

"I considered the horns, and, behold, there
came up among them another little horn, before
whom there were three of the first horns plucked
up by the roots: and, behold, in this horn were
eyes like the eyes of man, and a mouth speaking
great things" (Dan. 7:8).

Most Bible scholars agree that this fourth beast —
dreadful, terrible, and exceedingly strong as described by
Daniel— is symbolic of the great Roman Empire — an
empire that thrived nearly two thousand years ago but has
long since ceased to exist.

But then the Bible uses the strange term, *"and it had*
ten horns." What was Daniel referring to here? He said he
considered these horns, and then there came up another
little horn out of them. Just about every Bible scholar
agrees that these ten horns represent a reconstitution of the
old Roman Empire. In other words, the antichrist is going
to come out of the *area* of the old Roman Empire —
because it uses the term *"there came up among them*
another little horn." You have to focus on the two words
among them — and *them* refers to the nations of the old
Roman Empire boundaries.

Now we believe it is fairly obvious, from the Word of
God, that this great revival of the old Roman Empire is
going to become powerful, even dominant, during the last
days before Christ returns. The Roman Empire stretched all

the way from Great Britain to the Rhine River in Germany, down through parts of Eastern Europe into Turkey, and into the Middle East and Northern Africa. This is the area in question, and this is the area that is going to be militarily and socially critical in the end times (Dan. 7:19-22).

Daniel went on:

> *"And the ten horns out of this kingdom are ten kings that shall arise"* (Dan. 7:24).

This is, of course, speaking of future events. It was future in Daniel's day, and it is in the future still. Then Daniel went on to say, *"and another shall rise after them."* Of course, he is speaking of the antichrist. And that is the very *crux* of the question of Russia's role in the Middle East.

These ten horns represent ten kingdoms (ten nations), and these ten nations will be *in the territory* of the old Roman Empire. There is some difference of opinion among scholars. Some feel there will be a gigantic war fought, reducing the twenty-five or twenty-six nations that now occupy the old Roman Empire to ten nations. Of course, this would require that boundaries be altered and perhaps that names of nations be changed. Conversely, some think that just a part of the old Roman Empire area will supply these ten horns or ten nations. This is perhaps supported by the words *"out of this kingdom."* This would imply that *part* of the old Roman Empire territory would supply the ten nations of the antichrist.

But here's the point. There are *several* nations today within the area that once constituted the old Roman Empire *which are now controlled by the Soviet Union.* These are Albania, Romania, Bulgaria, Yugoslavia, and Hungary. They are known as the Balkans. Possibly all of these countries, or at least some of them, will be included in the

ten nations that are going to be taken over to form the
country of the antichrist shortly before the Second Coming
of Christ. Now the question must be asked: *How are these
countries going to be formed?*

Will Russia *voluntarily* give up her satellites — the
ones formerly included in the old Roman Empire? Knowing Soviet paranoia, it is doubtful she would do this
willingly. More than likely there will have to be a gigantic
war that will *force* the Soviet Union to relinquish control
over certain countries — which will then fall under the
antichrist's control. And it is in this roundabout manner
that the Bible makes its only reference to Russia's role in
this scenario.

NO ACTUAL BIBLICAL ACCOUNT
OF THE SOVIET UNION'S INVADING ISRAEL

I realize that some Bible students will question this
statement because many Christians believe that Ezekiel 38
is an account of the Soviet Union invading the Middle East
and Israel. Actually, Ezekiel is an account of the antichrist
(called Gog) who will gather his forces to come down on
Israel to totally annihilate her. He will, however, be
defeated by Almighty God.

> *"Son of man, set thy face against Gog, the
> land of Magog, the chief prince of Meshech and
> Tubal, and prophesy against him"* (Ezek. 38:2).

These three groups of people (or countries) are taken
by many to pertain to the Soviet Union. However, Magog,
Meshech, and Tubal were actually sons of Japheth who
became the Scythians, the Russians, and the Muscovites
— plus the Tiberenes and Cappadocians. In the Septuagint,
the word *rosh* is added to this list and convinces some that

this is Russia. Actually, the word *rosh* means "leader" or "chief."

So while many Bible students claim that Russia is specifically referred to here, she will actually only be *included* among these people, along with a number of other countries.

All of these people will, however, be under the control of Gog, the antichrist. These Bible statements prove only that Russia is *one* of the many nations that will be conquered by Gog and which will be under his command at the Battle of Armageddon (Dan. 11:44).

If one will read Daniel 11:44, one will see that the "north" referred to here is actually northern Europe plus Russia — and that the Soviet Union and her satellite nations will be defeated by Gog (the antichrist). He will subsequently command these as a *part* of the forces he will lead against Israel to produce the "final solution," or the complete annihilation of the Jews. Russia will *participate* under the antichrist, but that is as far as it will go.

Actually, Ezekiel 38 is an account of the antichrist who will come from Syria (which includes Lebanon, Syria, Iraq, and Iran today). It describes how he will lead many nations against Israel to completely destroy her.

GOG IS ACTUALLY THE ANTICHRIST.

Gog is not the title of the Soviet Union. It is the name of the antichrist — and Gog will not come from the Soviet Union. He can't possibly come from Russia. Scripture reveals that he will come from inside the old Roman Empire territory (Dan. 7:8-19, 25). These verses clearly state that he will come from the ten nations that will arise from within this area. Now, because Russia was never a part of the old Roman Empire — Russia will not be one of the ten nations from which the antichrist will arise. Therefore, the antichrist will not come from Russia.

And realizing this, it seems clear that for the ten nations to be formed inside the old Roman Empire that Russia must be defeated by the antichrist. This is because Russia controls several countries (named earlier) that were part of the old Roman Empire territory. These must then be liberated by the antichrist to complete the ten kingdoms mentioned by Daniel. There is, of course, a possibility that the Soviet Union *will* invade the Middle East independently — but if so, it will not really be fulfillment of any particular prophecy — Ezekiel 38 and 39.

THIS INVASION BY GOG
WILL *NOT* DESTROY ISRAEL.

Dark days are coming for Israel. She has had many hard times in the past, but the hardest of all are yet to come. I know this is difficult to accept, realizing the past problems endured, but the Bible says it will happen; and, without question, it will. This will occur during the Battle of Armageddon — which is depicted in Ezekiel 38 and 39 and in Zechariah 10 through 14.

During the Great Tribulation, yet to come, the Bible tells us that two-thirds of Israel will die. Most of this will no doubt occur during this great Battle of Armageddon (Zech. 13:8). The one-third that are left, however, will be brought through the fire as God refines them as silver and tries them as gold. His Word says this:

> *"They shall call on my name, and I will hear them: I will say, It is my people: and they shall say, The Lord is my God"* (Zech. 13:9).

It is of the great Battle of Armageddon (that will immediately precede the Second Coming of Christ) that God says:

> *"And it shall come to pass at the same time when Gog shall come against the land of Israel, saith the Lord God, that my fury shall come up in my face.*
>
> *"And I will rain upon him, and upon his bands, and upon the many people that are with him, an overflowing rain, and great hailstones, fire, and brimstone"* (Ezek. 38:18, 22).

This is where Gog, the antichrist, will be destroyed, along with his mighty armies, which will *include* the Soviet Union, plus Persia (Iran), Ethiopia, Libya, and Gomer, which is East Germany (Ezek. 38:5, 6). Scripture also adds that there will be additional nations aligned with the antichrist.

WILL THE UNITED STATES HELP ISRAEL IN THAT HOUR?

Every implication is that Israel will be alone, that no one will help her except God Almighty who will come in the person of the Lord Jesus Christ — and Ezekiel said His fury would come up in His face (Ezek. 38:18). The United States might possibly be there. I would hope and pray she would, but there is no biblical record of it.

Russia will meet her doom, but this will be *before* the Battle of Armageddon. As the ten countries (horns) are formed inside the old Roman Empire, tremendous fighting could result that will cause her to relinquish the countries mentioned earlier. This is where Russia will meet *her*

Armageddon. Just *how* it will happen, though, is not mentioned in the Bible. It could take place as the communist system falls apart from internal cancer — which might well occur as the result of a great war.

TO SUM UP

1. Communism, headed up by the Soviet Union, is Satan's political tool in the world today.

2. God hates this satanic political structure that has enslaved hundreds of millions.

3. Russia is definitely going to meet her doom. However, it would seem from Bible prophecy that her defeat will come in a series of events which will help bring on the rise of the antichrist.

4. There is no record in the Bible that Russia *per se* will invade Israel. It could happen, but the Bible is silent on the subject.

5. It would also seem from Bible prophecy that the fulfillment of Ezekiel 38 and 39 will be Gog (the antichrist) along with many nations, *including* the Soviet Union, which will come down to annihilate Israel once and for all. Russia's forces will no doubt be with him and will possibly aid and abet him greatly, but the antichrist will be the leader (Gog), and not some Soviet warlord.

6. In this final conflict, the antichrist, along with the Soviet Union and many other nations, will be totally and defeated, totally and completely.

And then the final mopping up will take place. Jesus Christ will return with His saints to reign supreme at the Battle of Armageddon. Communism and the Soviet Union will be no more. On the other hand, Israel — the tiny state, the people who have wandered in darkness for two thousand years — will come back home to the Lord Jesus Christ and will thereafter rule and reign with Him forever.

CHAPTER 8

THE ANTICHRIST

Little by little, whether the world realizes it or particularly *wants* it to happen, it is being informed of, and prepared for, the revelation of the antichrist. Hollywood has made a number of movies alluding to this individual who will have special powers from another world. His powers will be so extraordinary that modern man can scarcely comprehend their extent.

The spirit fostered and nurtured by Satan — that has prevailed since the fall of Adam and Eve in the Garden — is more evident today than ever before in the hearts and affairs of men. The spirit I refer to is that of the demagogue, the superego, the glorification of the flesh — of man desiring to elevate himself to the stature of God. This is, of course, the spirit of Satan, the spirit of darkness, the spirit of the antichrist.

History is spotted (and stained) with accounts of individuals who thought they could conquer the world: the Pharaohs, Darius the Persian, Cyrus the Mede, and Nebuchadnezzar. Then there was Alexander the Great — probably the most powerful of them all and perhaps the ancient role model, the prototype, of the antichrist himself. Subsequently, there were the Caesars who declared themselves to be gods. The world choked on its own blood during the blood-curdling conquests of Attila the Hun, Genghis Khan, Charlemagne, Napoleon, and perhaps worst of all — Adolf Hitler.

All these "world conquerors" have acted in the *spirit* of the antichrist. They were the forerunners and prototypes of this "man of sin" who will make the *final* attempt at complete world domination. The ambition of the individuals mentioned (plus many others not mentioned) was to do just that: to take over the whole world. They were all committed to placing the earth's population in subjugation to one individual. Most of them fell short of their goal, but they, nevertheless, tried.

These superegos, these demagogues, these individuals bigger than life (in their *own* eyes) thought they could accomplish *anything*. And this same spirit is rushing pell-mell toward a course of destruction that will obscure and overshadow any previous exercise in world annihilation. We are speaking, of course, of the Great Tribulation period when Satan makes his final bid for world dominance. He will do it through the one commonly referred to as the antichrist.

WHO IS THE ANTICHRIST?

The antichrist is scripturally referred to by a number of names and titles. In I John 2:18 he is called the *"antichrist."* In Isaiah 10:20-27 and Micah 5:3-15 he is called the *"Assyrian."* In Isaiah 14:4 he is called the *"king of Babylon."* In other places Isaiah refers to him as the *"spoiler"* and the *"extortioner."*

In Ezekiel 38:2, 3 he is called *"Gog, the chief prince of Meshech and Tubal."* This may well be the title he will adopt during the Great Tribulation period. Daniel, of course, calls him the *"little horn"* as well as the *"king of fierce countenance."* Daniel also refers to him as the *"prince that shall come"* and the *"king of the north."* Paul calls him the *"man of sin,"* the *"son of perdition,"* and *"that Wicked one."* Finally, he is called the *"beast"* by Daniel and by John as well in the book of Revelation.

The antichrist (or beast) will be a mortal, a human being. We know this because he will *die* at Armageddon. Angels don't die, and so, of course, Satan cannot die. A resurrected human cannot die, because *all* resurrected individuals — whether they be the righteous at the first resurrection or the wicked at the second resurrection (of damnation) — will be *made* immortal and cannot die. They will exist forever, either in the pit of hell or in the glories of God. Therefore, the errant doctrine that the antichrist will be a *resurrected* human being, risen to become mortal again (and to die again on earth in his second lifetime), is not to be found in the Word of God. So we know from this that the antichrist will not be Judas, Antiochus Epiphanes, or any other man one might choose to imagine filling this abominable role.

Still some do erroneously teach that the antichrist will be a *reincarnated* being. In other words, one who lived as some *other* being (such as Judas, Attila the Hun, or perhaps Alexander the Great) and who will now be reincarnated as the *beast*. This is not taught in the Word of God. Reincarnation is unscriptural and is nowhere suggested in the Bible. This also is, therefore, impossible.

The antichrist will be called *Prince of Grecia,* but this does not mean he will be Alexander the Great reincarnated. It concerns the final vision of Daniel regarding the Grecian Empire. It refers to the four divisions of Alexander's empire, ruled by four Grecian generals after the death of Alexander. The antichrist will emerge from one of these political units. He will come from the *Syrian* division of the old Grecian Empire (Dan. 8:8-26; 9:20-27; 11:36-45).

It is important to realize that the antichrist is, as we have previously mentioned, a man. At the time of this writing, he is unknown. In other words, he is not someone now prominent in world affairs. He might well be *alive* today, but nothing definite is known of him, nor is he prominent in world affairs that we know of at this time.

WHEN WILL HE MAKE HIS DEBUT?

Naturally, we do not know — insofar as year, month, or day is concerned — just *when* the antichrist will make his debut on the world stage. We do know, however, that certain events must occur *before* he comes upon the scene. Paul is very specific about this:

> *"And now ye know what withholdeth that he might be revealed in his time"* (II Thes. 2:6).

Of course, the word "withholdeth" refers to the church of the Living God, here on earth at this moment, a tremendous bulwark against the powers of darkness. Then Paul uses the phrase *"that he might be revealed in his time,"* speaking of the antichrist who will come upon the world scene. Paul goes on to explain:

> *"For the mystery of iniquity doth already work: only he who now letteth will let, until he be taken out of the way"* (II Thes. 2:7).

This is speaking of the body of Christ, the church, which will be *taken out of the way* as the rapture takes place. There are basically three influences that inhibit lawlessness. The first one is government. We know, however, that government will be very much apparent during the reign of the antichrist, when government will be revealed (even as it sometimes is today) as a *hotbed* of lawlessness — rather than an inhibiting influence.

The second factor *could* be the Holy Spirit. (It is a widely taught fact that the Holy Spirit will be removed from the world at the rapture.) Actually, this is not scripturally possible, for the Bible tells us *He* (the Holy Spirit) will be here on the earth all through the Great Tribulation — and actually forever (John 14:16; Acts 2:16-21; Rev. 12:17; 19:10; and others).

So the only counterinfluence to lawlessness that could be taken out of this world is the church of the Living God. It will, of course, be raptured before the advent of the antichrist, and is the *only* one of the potential hinderers of lawlessness that *will* be removed from the earth (I Thes. 4:16).

Next, Paul goes on to say:

> *"And then shall that Wicked be revealed"*
> (II Thes. 2:8).

Now I think a careful reading of this makes it completely evident that the antichrist will *not* be revealed until *after* the rapture takes place. Verse 7 talks about the church being taken out of the way (which is what we refer to as the rapture) and verse 8 uses the term *"and then shall that Wicked be revealed."* Of course, the *Wicked* is the antichrist:

> *". . . whom the Lord shall consume with the spirit of his mouth, and shall destroy with the brightness of his coming"* (II Thes. 2:8).

This will take place at the Battle of Armageddon.

We also realize that the antichrist will not come on the scene until after ten kingdoms are formed within the old Roman Empire territory (Dan. 7:23, 24). However, before we investigate this matter of the formation of the ten kingdoms, let's go on to our next point.

WHERE WILL HE COME FROM?

Daniel wrote down what he saw:

> *"After this I saw in the night visions, and behold a fourth beast, dreadful and terrible, and strong exceedingly; and it had great iron teeth: it devoured and brake in pieces, and stamped the residue with the feet of it: and it was diverse from all the beasts that were before it; and it had ten horns"* (Dan. 7:7).

This fourth beast is the symbol of the old Roman Empire that existed during the Master's day and also during the time in which John wrote the book of Revelation. Actually, the Roman Empire (symbolized by the dreadful, exceedingly strong beast with the great iron teeth) lasted for nearly a thousand years — longer than any other government on the face of the earth.

A very unique beast, there is nothing on earth with which one can compare it. It is a dreadful, exceedingly strong beast with great iron teeth. This represents (as does the iron of the image of Daniel 2:40-43) the long-term *strength* of the Roman nation. Prophetically, and in actuality, it devoured all other beasts and stamped on them with its feet — meaning that it conquered all the territories of the first three beasts, which were Medo-Persia, Babylon, and Greece. It was different from all the beasts before it, not only in its utilization of a republican form of government, but also in power, greatness, extent of dominion, and period of domination.

The latter part of Daniel 7:7 uses the term *"and it had ten horns."* Even though this is connected with the vision Daniel saw, it has nothing whatever to do with the great Roman Empire. It symbolizes the kingdoms which will, in the last days, rise up. These will actually be a latter-day *reproduction* of the old Roman Empire — or as some refer to it, a *revised* rather than a *revived* Roman Empire. The reason the term "horn" is used in the Word of God is because horns are always symbolic of kings and seats of power. Because the horns were the last parts of the beasts described by Daniel, we will also consider them last here:

> *"I considered the horns, and, behold, there came up among them another little horn, before whom there were three of the first horns plucked up by the roots: and, behold, in this horn were eyes like the eyes of man, and a mouth speaking great things"* (Dan. 7:8).

Here Scripture uses the term *little horn* to refer to the antichrist. This *little horn* comes up last — after the ten horns are fully grown. Then it mentions that this *little horn* plucks three of the ten horns up by the roots, symbolizing the antichrist coming in the days of the ten kingdoms within the boundaries of the old Roman Empire. This simply means that the antichrist will declare war on these three countries (Egypt, Greece, and Turkey) and overthrow them, and the other seven will then submit to him without further resistance. So, the *little horn* — the antichrist — will be a man who will speak blasphemies against God.

When we carefully consider verses 7 and 8, we see clearly that they say *"there came up among them another little horn."* The words *"among them"* used here are speaking of the ten kingdoms that will be formed inside the old Roman Empire. So, we know from Daniel 7:7, 8 that the *little horn* (antichrist) must come from within the old Roman Empire territory.

By referring to a map, we see that this area included France, Lebanon, Turkey, Egypt, Israel, Italy, Syria, Libya, Yugoslavia, Bulgaria, Romania, and Greece — plus other countries. And it is apparent that it is from these countries that the antichrist will appear because of the term *"there came up among them."* (One can refer to a map of the old Roman Empire territory that existed during the time of Christ to see the exact boundaries.)

Daniel 8 further specifies the area from whence the antichrist will arise. We saw in the preceding passages that the antichrist has to come from the territory of the old Roman Empire. Now Daniel narrows it down even further, when he states:

> *"Therefore the he goat waxed very great: and when he was strong, the great horn was broken; and for it [in its place] came up four notable ones toward the four winds of heaven"* (Dan. 8:8).

Oddly enough, in this passage Daniel is speaking of the empire that was in power *before* the great Roman Empire came into being. The "he goat" is symbolic of the Grecian Empire headed up by Alexander the Great. The term *"when he was strong"* refers to Alexander's strength at the time he was conquering all that lay before him. Then it says *"the great horn was broken,"* referring to the death of Alexander when he was only thirty-three.

Next it uses the term *"and for it came up four notable ones toward the four winds of heaven."* This prophesied that four of Alexander's generals would divide his empire into four empires referred to today as Greece, Turkey, Syria, and Egypt. We know this from the boundary lines of that time and those of today.

Then Daniel narrows down even further the exact source of the antichrist:

> *"And out of one of them came forth a little horn, which waxed exceeding great, toward the south, and toward the east, and toward the pleasant land"* (Dan. 8:9).

The term *"out of one of them"* means that out of one of these empires claimed by the four generals who survived politically after Alexander's death will come the *little horn*. These countries are now Greece, Turkey, Syria, and Egypt. So we know that from one of these countries will come the antichrist because of the phrase *"out of one of them came forth a little horn."* The term *little horn* speaks of the antichrist.

In Daniel 11 so much graphic detail is given concerning what is now ancient history that many Bible scholars felt for a long time that Daniel couldn't have written the book that bears his name. It was too graphic, too exact, too perfect. It left absolutely nothing to one's imagination, as if someone read the pages of history *after* all these things came about — rather than prophesying them beforehand.

Of course, archaeological findings have since proved that Daniel did write the book bearing his name and that he wrote it, with God's anointing, long before the actual events took place. The tremendous detail in chapter 11 was simply the Spirit of prophecy that came upon him, with God giving him myriad details which were to prove extremely important to the country of Israel. Today one can go to the library and check out books dealing with the development of the old Grecian Empire under Alexander the Great and confirm his death and the subsequent division of his empire by his four generals. The status of these four generals was foretold by the term found in Daniel 8:8, *"four notable ones."*

Then it speaks, over and over again, of the *"king of the south"* and *"king of the north."* The term *"king of the north"* is used about six times in Daniel 11 alone. As any history book will tell you, it's not speaking of the Soviet Union — it has nothing to do with the Russia of today. When Daniel uses the term *"king of the north,"* he refers to *"north of the pleasant land"* — which is Israel.

When Daniel uses the term *"king of the south"* (as he does repeatedly in the eleventh chapter), he means *south of Israel*. And, once again, this speaks of the four kingdoms that were formed by Alexander's generals. The *"king of the north"* refers to Syria, while the *"king of the south"* refers to Egypt.

This is all history. You can pick up a book from your local library concerning Greek and Roman history and all of this will be present, down to the minutest detail, just as Daniel prophesied it hundreds of years earlier. Cleopatra of Egypt rose to power in one of these countries evolving from the Alexandrian Empire. She was, of course, made famous in recent years by a Hollywood portrayal of her in a much-publicized movie.

THE ANTICHRIST WILL COME FROM SYRIA.

In Daniel 11:40 the phrase is used, *"And at the time of the end."* This speaks of the fulfillment of the reason for Daniel's vision. It concerns the very end of the Gentile world power, symbolized by the *image* of Daniel 2 and the *beast* of Daniel 7 and 8 (also recorded in Revelation 13:17 and other Scriptures that could be named). It refers to the Great Tribulation period — the time of the end — and uses the term *"shall the king of the south push at him."* "Him" refers here to the antichrist, and the *"king of the south"* refers to Egypt. It simply means that the king of the south (which is Egypt) will push against the king of the north (which is Syria and the antichrist).

Daniel 11:44 says *"he."* This "he" shall enter into the glorious land. The glorious land is Israel. This simply means that after the antichrist from Syria has conquered Greece, Turkey, and Egypt, that the rest of the seven countries (as mentioned elsewhere in this chapter) forming the revised Roman Empire will give their power to him. At this point he (the antichrist) will break his covenant with the Jews and enter the glorious land — endeavoring to destroy all Jews and taking Israel for his very own. This will climax in the Battle of Armageddon — which we will discuss a little later on.

So now we find out exactly where the antichrist will come from; he will come from Syria. However, there is something here we must understand. The "Syria" spoken of at that particular time included our *present-day* Syria, Lebanon, Irac, Iran, and even parts of Pakistan. In other words, the boundaries of the countries of that day were cuite a bit larger than present-day Greece, Syria, Egypt, Turkey, etc.

The main point to be remembered is that the king of the north is not Russia, has nothing to do with Russia, and has never referred to Russia. It simply speaks (as we have briefly outlined what the Bible gives in great detail) of the breaking up of the old Alexandrian Empire. It uses the term (as we mentioned earlier) *"and out of one of them"* — the term "them" meaning Syria, Turkey, Greece, and Egypt. Then, when we read over and over again, *"the king of the north,"* we realize from the description given — and from history — that it is speaking of Syria.

Once again I want to emphasize that when we think of Syria, we shouldn't think of the present-day borders of Syria. These *are* quite large in comparison to Israel, but quite small in comparison to the Syria existing some 2,200 years ago. To pinpoint even further, we personally feel that the antichrist will come from one of these countries representing ancient Syria.

So we see from Daniel's writing that the antichrist will come from a part of the world prominent in today's headlines. At the time of this writing, Iraq and Iran are in conflict. These two countries control tremendous reserves of oil — oil that will fuel the fires of the antichrist's bid for world power. Perhaps even more importantly, they could *finance* his efforts to rule planet earth.

Now let's look at the *goal* of the *"king of the north."*

WHAT IS HIS GOAL?

The antichrist, *"the king of the north,"* will desire to rule the entire world and will be inspired by Satan to do this. He will be aided and abetted by a fallen angel (who we will discuss momentarily) as well as by Satan himself. It will be basically *Satan's last bid* for world domination. There has never been anything like it in the history of man, and there never *will* be anything like it again. It is the time referred to as *"Jacob's trouble."*

Now, the question must be asked: Will he be successful in his bid for world domination? Many Bible teachers declare that he will rule the entire planet, governing every country on the face of the earth and forcing every person to take his mark. Those who do not take his mark will be executed or face dire personal and economic consequences. Is this the way it will be? Let's first investigate some of the resources he will have at his disposal.

"The beast that thou sawest was, and is not; and shall ascend out of the bottomless pit, and go into perdition: and they that dwell on the earth shall wonder . . . they behold the beast that was, and is not, and yet is" (Rev. 17:8).

The latter portion of this verse is a complicated statement that most people do not understand. First of all, when it speaks of the beast *"that thou sawest,"* it is not speaking of the antichrist. The term "beast" is used interchangeably for a number of evil beings, as well as some of the angelic beings in the portals of Glory. It *also* refers to the antichrist. It is something of a generic term.

When John used the term "was" in verse 8, he was referring to the supernatural angel who was one of Satan's lieutenants (a fallen angel) who aided and abetted Alexander the Great in his tremendous conquest and rise to power. The world couldn't at that time understand how Alexander the Great, in such a short time and at such a young age (he died at thirty-three), could accomplish all he did. He repeatedly defeated armies many times the size of his own. His strategies were so innovative and effective that none could stand against him. His tactics are even studied today. Of course, the *secret* of all this was the unseen demonic being. Even Alexander was unaware of his existence, yet he assisted Alexander in the many conquests that resulted in world domination (the world of that day).

When John used the term *"and is not,"* he simply meant that Alexander the Great was dead at the moment of John's writing and that his kingdom had passed on into oblivion. The Roman Empire had now taken over and this angelic being (who had helped Alexander) was not *then* present to help anyone. (You can find further reference to this in Daniel 10:12-14; 10:20.)

WHO WILL AID HIM?

John, in using the term *"and shall ascend out of the bottomless pit,"* was speaking of this fallen angel who helped Alexander the Great — who will come out of the bottomless pit again during the Great Tribulation period to aid the antichrist just as he helped Alexander the Great so many centuries before. Of course, the world will be unaware of his existence. He will be, however, the cause of many of the antichrist's triumphs.

Finally, John closes verse 8 by saying *"was"* — speaking of the days when this fallen angel helped Alexander the Great. John used the term *"and is not,"* which speaks of the time when John lived and wrote the book of Revelation. This would be two thousand years ago, and Alexander's fallen angel was *not* currently aiding or abetting anyone *at that specific moment.* He was then in the bottomless pit. He used the term *"and yet is"* to denote that he would come again, at a later time, to perform the specific work that had been prophesied. The false prophet (beast) as is recorded in Revelation 13:11-13 will probably be aided by this fallen angel.

So, the antichrist will be aided by all the powers of hell. In other words, Satan will pull out all the stops. The brightest and most powerful of the fallen angels will aid and abet him in his bid for world domination. Daniel goes on to tell exactly what he will do and the type of characteristics that will identify him.

Daniel 7:20 speaks of *"ten horns that were in his head."* This refers to the ten nations which will make up the *new* (revised) Roman Empire — nations he will defeat or nations that will give their power to him. Then it uses the term, *"the other which came up,"* referring to *the little horn* which will dominate all these powers — *"and before whom three fell,"* referring to the three (Turkey, Greece, and Egypt) who will declare war on the antichrist, but who will be totally defeated by him. The other seven will then *give* their power unto him.

Going further, the term is used: *"that horn that had eyes, and a mouth that spake very great things, whose look was more stout than his fellows."* This simply implies more power or might. He will be greater than other rulers of the earth — more powerful than other kings — simply because he will be aided and abetted by this fallen angel. In addition, he will be further supported by Satan himself.

We can already sense the spirit of darkness pervading the world — a spirit that is in total opposition to all that is good, decent, noble, honest, holy, and true. In other words, it's a spirit against God, and one that will reach its culmination under the antichrist. Then this antichrist spirit will permeate and pervade all seats of power: the government, public schools, education, television, the media — every agency capable of influencing men's minds against God, His Bible, and all those who live for Him. The Bible even uses the phrase that he *"shall wear out the saints"* (Dan. 7:25).

In Daniel 8:11 we see that the antichrist will show his true colors, revealing his personal obsession to be God. As all potentates have done, his picture will constantly appear throughout the world, in newspapers and on television. His inflamed ego will know no bounds. Were you to go today into Cuba, China, the Soviet Union, or other communistic countries (or any country ruled by a dictator, for that matter) you would find it impossible to escape constant exposure to images of the leaders of these countries. This is the spirit of the antichrist at work even today. It has always been with us, but it will reach a crescendo during the days of the Great Tribulation period — when he will magnify himself as no man has ever before promoted himself.

Daniel 8 speaks of his power being so great that few will oppose him:

> *"He shall destroy wonderfully, and shall prosper, and practise"* (Dan. 8:24).

> *"He shall cause craft to prosper"* (Dan. 8:25).

The term "craft" is not used in the "arts and crafts" sense. It means *deceit*. In other words, he will be *crafty*. Craftiness, or deceit, will become a powerful weapon in his hands as hundreds of millions will be deceived as he magnifies himself in his heart. In verse 25 Daniel states,

> *"By peace shall [he] destroy many."*

"NEITHER SHALL HE REGARD THE GOD OF HIS FATHERS, NOR THE DESIRE OF WOMEN" (DAN. 11:37).

This is a strange term to use: *"the desire of women."* It is actually speaking of the Lord Jesus Christ — that He was born of the Virgin Mary. The antichrist will do everything possible to deny and suppress this fact.

> *"Nor regard any god: for he shall magnify himself above all"* (Dan. 11:37).

The term *"for he shall magnify himself above all"* reveals that he will magnify himself even above the Lord Jesus Christ. He will not consider Jesus Christ to be the Son of God. He will even attempt to change our present method of reckoning time — B.C. and A.D. — referring to the periods before and after the birth of Christ.

"But in his estate shall he honour the God of forces: and a god whom his fathers knew not shall he honour with gold, and silver, and with precious stones, and pleasant things" (Dan. 11:38).

War will be his god, and he will seek to conquer the entire earth.

WHAT WILL HAPPEN TO HIM?

There are many people who teach that the antichrist will rule the entire world. Some may ask the question: "Will he rule the United States and Canada as well? What about Central and South America and other parts of the world?" The Bible is fairly specific as to the territory he will conquer and rule. We know, first of all, that there are some countries that will escape (this is referred to in Daniel 11:41 where it says that Edom, Moab, and the children of Ammon shall escape). This refers, within the geography of today, to Jordan.

We believe the manner of his actual debut will follow a scenario something like this: ancient Babylon will be rebuilt (Zech. 5:5-11; Rev. 18:3-10) and the antichrist will reign from restored Babylon (which is in Iraq) for the first three and one-half years of the Tribulation period, while he solidifies his power (Isa. 14:4-17).

The antichrist will make a "non-aggression pact" with Israel, which will guarantee Israel's protection from other Arab powers — or from anyone else for that matter. He will then break this treaty with Israel and enter Judea to take over Jerusalem and make it his capital. The Jewish temple will serve as his capitol building (Dan. 9:27; 11:40-45; II Thes. 2:4; Rev. 11:1, 2; 12:1-17).

Israel will accept him as the Messiah in fulfillment of the Master's prophecy in John where Jesus said:

> *"I am come in my Father's name, and ye receive me not: if another shall come in his own name, him ye will receive"* (John 5:43).

The word "another," which He uses here, refers to the antichrist. The Jews will receive the antichrist as their Messiah, but he will show his true colors at the midpoint of the Tribulation period, at which time he will come upon Israel to completely destroy her. He will not succeed in this, but he will come very close.

WHERE WILL HE REIGN FROM?

Jerusalem will be made his capital city and he will erect a statue of himself in the temple, commanding individuals to bow down before it. This is, of course, the *"abomination of desolation"* that Daniel speaks of in Daniel 9:27. The antichrist will be totally committed to the destruction of Israel, even to the point of pursuing them into Petra where it is believed a remnant will flee.

But then, we are told:

> *"But tidings out of the east and out of the north shall trouble him"* (Dan. 11:44).

He will thus have to turn his attention away from the eradication of Israel and deal with these problems from the east and the north. The east and the north referred to here simply mean east and north of his empire. We know the countries lying to the east and north of his empire are China, Japan, Russia, Poland, etc. So from this we know that the antichrist will declare war on the Soviet Union and possibly Japan and China at this time. They will realize that he is endeavoring to assume control of the world and will set out to derail his plans. Of course, they will not succeed and he will defeat them. Consecuently, his preoccupation with these events will spare Israel from complete annihilation.

WILL HE CONQUER THE WORLD?

Once again, we can tell from these particular Scriptures that the antichrist will not totally concuer the world. There is no record anywhere within the prophecies of God's Holy Word that he will concuer the United States of America.

There is a possibility that the United States will endeavor to help Israel during this time, but there is no actual evidence (scripturally speaking) whether she will or not. We further read from the Word of God that he will *not* rule from Washington, D.C., Rome, etc., but will have two capitals during his reign — Babylon and Jerusalem. He will reign from Babylon for the first three and one-half years and from Jerusalem for the second three and one-half years.

We're given another Scripture in the Word of God that lets us know he *will not* succeed in his bid for world domination:

> *"But the judgment shall sit [which refers to God Almighty along with the holy angels], and they shall take away his dominion, to consume and to destroy it unto the end"* (Dan. 7:26).

So, like all other ambitious world concuerors, the antichrist will fall short of concuering the entire world. He will not succeed in his obsession to do so.

WHAT WILL BE HIS MARK?

In the nations he *does* conquer, he will institute his mark:

> *"And he causeth all, both small and great, rich and poor, free and bond, to receive a mark in their right hand, or in their foreheads:*
> *"And that no man might buy or sell, save he that had the mark, or the name of the beast, or the number of his name"* (Rev. 13:16, 17).

From this terminology, we don't really know what his mark will be. Neither do we know what his name is. We do know that the *number* of his name (using Hebrew numerology) is 666 because John tells us:

> *"For it is the number of a man; and his number is Six hundred threescore and six"* (Rev. 13:18).

In every land that the antichrist conquers, he will demand that all who do not take his mark either be killed or otherwise persecuted. From this fact, some feel that his rule will encompass the entire planet, but there are many specific Scriptures, as we have outlined, stating the opposite. Admittedly, if God did not stop him, he *would* conquer the whole earth. That will be his plan and his desire, but he will be denied his great ambition.

The reason he will fall short of world domination is simply because:

> *"He shall also stand up against the Prince of princes; but he shall be broken without hand"* (Dan. 8:25).

This is when he goes too far. He will stand up against the First and the Last, the Alpha and the Omega, the Prince of princes — and he shall be broken without hand. God will break him with little difficulty. This is where he meets his match. This is when he finally goes too far.

You see — when the antichrist sets up his image in the temple in Jerusalem, when he makes the city of the King his capital, when he plants the tabernacle of his palace in the glorious, holy mountain — that's when he oversteps his bounds. He will come to the end as Daniel foretold:

"And none shall help him" (Dan. 11:45).

It is here that the antichrist comes up against the *real* "heavy-weight champion of the universe." This is when God pulls off His gloves and all heaven literally breaks loose. We are told exactly how it will end.

THE GRAND FINALE

Daniel 7:11 tells us that the antichrist will be killed and his body destroyed and given to burning flame. Then, in Ezekiel 38, it gives the account of his demise. God Almighty says here:

"I am against thee, O Gog, the chief prince of Meshech and Tubal:
"And I will turn thee back, and put hooks into thy jaws, and I will bring thee forth, and all thine army, horses and horsemen, all of them clothed with all sorts of armour, even a great company with bucklers and shields, all of them handling swords" (Ezek. 38:3, 4).

"Thou [the antichrist] shalt ascend and

*come like a storm, thou shalt be like a cloud to
cover the land, thou, and all thy bands, and
many people with thee"* (Ezek. 38:9).

The antichrist, after conquering the Soviet Union (plus
China and Japan and many other countries) will come
down on Israel for the "final solution." He will attempt
what Hitler could not do. He will think, as Ezekiel reports
in chapter 38, verse 10, *"an evil thought."* In verse 15 it
says he will come *"out of the north parts."* This is not
speaking of the Soviet Union, but of the old Syrian area. He
will come again from Babylon to destroy Israel, once and
for all.

He will cover the land like a cloud, and verse 16 says,
"it shall be in the latter days." When this happens, God
promises that *"my fury shall come up in my face"* (verse
18). Then, God says:

*"I will rain upon him, and upon his bands,
and upon the many people that are with him, an
overflowing rain, and great hailstones, fire, and
brimstone"* (Ezek. 38:22).

*"I will turn thee back, and leave but the sixth
part of thee, and will cause thee to come up from
the north parts, and will bring thee upon the
mountains of Israel:*

*"Thou shalt fall upon the mountains of
Israel, thou, and all thy bands, and the people
that is with thee: I will give thee unto the ravenous birds of every sort, and to the beasts of the
field to be devoured.*

"For I have spoken it, saith the Lord God"
(Ezek. 39:2, 4, 5).

This is where the antichrist will meet his destruction. He will meet the Lord Jesus Christ as the Master returns from heaven — accompanied by all the saints of God. The Lord will *"fight as in the days of old"* and completely subdue the antichrist. It is the final solution — but not quite as the antichrist had anticipated it. It will be *his* final solution, however.

This will end all bids for world domination by all the prospective world dictators of the ages. At this point, Jesus will set up His millennial kingdom in the city of Jerusalem and with the saints of God will rule and reign for a thousand years. After this will come *"the new heavens and the new earth."*

> *"He which testifieth these things saith, Surely I come quickly . . . Even so, come, Lord Jesus"* (Rev. 22:20).

CHAPTER 9

THE BATTLE OF ARMAGEDDON

"And the sixth angel poured out his vial upon the great river Euphrates; and the water thereof was dried up, that the way of the kings of the east might be prepared.

"And I saw three unclean spirits like frogs come out of the mouth of the dragon, and out of the mouth of the beast, and out of the mouth of the false prophet.

"For they are the spirits of devils, working miracles, which go forth unto the kings of the earth and of the whole world, to gather them to the battle of that great day of God Almighty.

"Behold, I come as a thief. Blessed is he that watcheth, and keepeth his garments, lest he walk naked, and they see his shame.

"And he gathered them together into a place called in the Hebrew tongue Armageddon" (Rev. 16:12-16).

MEGIDDO

Some time ago I had the opportunity to stand amid the ruins of the ancient city of Megiddo.

This ancient city is located six miles southwest of Mount Carmel. It was the capital of the portion of Canaan given to Joshua, as described in Joshua 12:21; 17:11; and Judges 1:27. Its position dominates the entrance to a pass crossing the Carmel Mountain range on the route between Asia and Africa. It is the keystone of the area encompassed by the Euphrates and Nile rivers, and has been the scene of many battles through the ages. Thothmes III, founder of an ancient dynasty, said, "Megiddo is worth a thousand cities."

As I stood gazing over the beautiful valley of Jehoshaphat (Megiddo), I realized that it must be one of the most beautiful sights in the world. Crops grow there year-round and it stretches almost as far as the eye can see. As I stood there amid its ancient ruins, I was overwhelmed by a sense of peace, serenity, and heavenly calm.

At the same time, however, I realized that the very heavens above me would, in the near future, be ripped asunder by the coming of our Lord and Saviour, Jesus Christ. I realized that every saint of God who has ever lived — from the time of Adam until this very moment — will come back with the Lord Jesus Christ. I realized that this peaceful valley, spread out before me like a beautiful painting, would soon be filled with tanks and screaming jets, as the mightiest army ever known to the world (and under the direction of the antichrist) invades to create the great prophetic Battle of Armageddon. This is where it will all take place.

The name "Armageddon" is becoming more prominent in newscasts and the fast-paced order of events of today. The late General Douglas MacArthur said that the next great conflict might well prove to be Armageddon. He meant, of course, the word "Armageddon" as a figure of speech, a metaphor. He was implying that modern weaponry had reached such a destructive level that it could very well spell the end of the human race — if total war were to lead to *use* of the ultimate weapons now at our disposal.

What will actually happen *at* Armageddon? What will precede and signal this terrible struggle? *When* will it happen? Let's look at the order of events leading up to this greatest conflict the world has ever known. The Bible lays it all out for us in chronological order.

1. RAPTURE

The rapture will be the most earth-shaking event in the history of the world. It could take place at any moment (I Thes. 4:16, 17). There are no Scriptures yet to be fulfilled before *this* awesome event, but there are a *number* of Scriptures to be fulfilled before the Lord's Second Coming. Paul told us about the rapture in I Thessalonians 4:16. It will attract the world's attention as nothing else could. The instantaneous disappearance of multiplied millions of people — from every nation on the face of the earth — will capture headlines as no other event in history.

2. GREAT TRIBULATION PERIOD

At this point the world will be plunged into the Great Tribulation period. Jesus called it:

> ". . . *great tribulation, such as was not since the beginning of the world to this time, no, nor ever shall be*" (Matt. 24:21).

If we pause to review history and think of Attila the Hun, Genghis Khan, Adolf Hitler, Joseph Stalin, and all the other despots of the ages, it's hard to comprehend that coming events are going to be worse. But worse they *shall* be. The words of our very Lord confirm this, so we can be sure that this will be a horrible period indeed. *During* the Great Tribulation period the antichrist will make his public debut and try for world domination. And then will come the battle.

3. THE BATTLE OF ARMAGEDDON

Let's look at the principal cast of characters in this scenario as the Bible outlines them for us.

The person popularly and commonly referred to by Christians as "the antichrist" is called by *various* names throughout the Word of God. He is called the *"beast,"* the *"man of sin,"* the *"son of perdition,"* the *"little horn,"* and the *"antichrist."*

The antichrist will be a man, not some reincarnated individual who has lived in the past (such as Judas, Attila the Hun, Adolf Hitler, or other personalities dredged up from profane history). He will be a man who becomes famous and powerful, with one desire before him — total domination of the world. The antichrist will not succeed in his effort; he will be stopped short of his goal.

The Bible tells us:

> *"He [the antichrist] shall also stand up against the Prince of princes"* (Dan. 8:25).

This, of course, refers to our Lord, Jesus Christ. *"But,"* we are assured, *"he [the antichrist] shall be broken without hand."* He emphatically will *not* succeed in his efforts to dominate the world. He will conquer many nations — and overrun many empires — but *some* will escape (Dan. 11:41).

Of course, the question must be asked, "Will the United States be overrun by the antichrist, and will it *oppose* him?" It is impossible to answer these questions specifically because the Bible does not address them directly.

As we have mentioned previously, the Bible is a Jewish book. It would seem that, basically, God addresses other nations only as they relate to Israel. We would go a step further and say that He seems to relate to other nations only when Israel is being severely punished. Naturally, the United States of America is very much intertwined with Israel today, and Israel's position is very weak. However, even though the danger is very real, it is more of a threatening nature than anything else. So, it would seem that due to Israel's relative safety today, even though she is in an unstable position, that God did not see fit in His Word to relate to this specific time in Israel's history.

So, the United States is not actually mentioned in Bible prophecy. I realize that many contend that the antichrist will control the entire world, but the Bible does not say this. It *limits* his kingdom, basically, to the area of the old Roman Empire.

We are told in Daniel 7:7 that the great Roman Empire will rise again. It is described as a beast, dreadful and terrible and exceedingly strong. In the latter portion of verse 7 it states, *"and it had ten horns."* It uses the term *"little horn"* in the middle of the eighth verse. This refers to the antichrist.

Daniel then goes on to tell how the antichrist will *defeat* three of the nations comprising the revived Roman Empire, while the other seven will actually *give* their kingdoms to him (Dan. 7:8; Rev. 17:12-14). This will be the basis for his empire until he starts to expand by military means, perhaps defeating even such powers as Soviet Russia, China, and Japan in the process.

Daniel 7:24 refers to *"the ten horns."* Most Bible scholars see these as the ten nations arising as the restored (or revised) Roman Empire. These would logically include the area encompassed by the *old* Roman Empire and would today include Poland, Czechoslovakia, parts of Germany, Libya, Italy, and other parts of Europe, plus parts of the Middle East.

It then goes on to speak (in the latter part of verse 24 and in verse 25) of the antichrist arising out of these kingdoms. In other words, he will come from somewhere within this area. He definitely will *not* come from the United States or the Soviet Union, nor will he come from China or any of the eastern nations.

In Daniel 8 we are given a more specific indication of his origin. The ninth verse says, *"And out of one of them came forth a little horn."* The *"one of them"* refers to the four kingdoms that developed from Alexander the Great's empire.

Following this, the Bible tells us:

> *"And the king of the north shall come against him like a whirlwind"* (Dan. 11:40).

In Daniel 11:41 the antichrist is *"enter[ing] into the glorious land,"* which is Israel. So we know from all this that the king of the north is Syria, and we can conclude that the antichrist will come from Syria. You must understand, however, that the Syria referred to here is not precisely the Syria we know today. Present-day Syria is much smaller than it was when Daniel wrote these words (under the anointing of the Holy Spirit). Syria then embraced not only present-day Syria, but also parts of what are now Lebanon, Iraq, and Iran. So, the antichrist could come from anywhere in this area and still fulfill Bible prophecy concerning the king of the north (Syria).

ISRAEL

Next, let's look at the cast of characters who will perform in this grand scenario *composed by God* for the last days. When you mention Israel, you are talking about God's chosen people. These strange people have played a major part in influencing the course of world history.

They sprang from the loins of Abraham. The Mosaic law was delivered to them as the foundation of *all* law on the face of the earth today. Through them came the Branch, the Vine, the Son of David, the Messiah — the Lord Jesus Christ — and yet they rejected Him. This wonderful, strange, *glorious* people — after their rejection of the Lord Jesus Christ — saw their city of Jerusalem utterly destroyed by the Roman armies of Titus in 70 A.D. At this point in history they were scattered over the face of the earth — exactly as Daniel said they would be. In chapter 9 Daniel stated that the Messiah would come and be cut off (verse 26). Then he spoke of the Romans who would come and destroy the city and the sanctuary — which they did in 70 A.D.

There's one thing that must be remembered about the book of Daniel and the book of Revelation — they are composed of a basically Jewish cast of characters. Most everything pertains to the Jews; most everything pertains to Israel. God's dealings with the human race are always influenced by *how they affect Israel*.

The entirety of the book of Revelation will *influence* the whole earth, but basically it has two primary purposes: *one,* for God to pour out His judgment on a world that has forgotten Him days without number, and, *two,* to bring His chosen people, the Jews, back to Him.

The Jews have strayed and wandered for many long years. The Master himself told them:

> *"O . . . thou that killest the prophets, and stonest them which are sent unto thee, how often would I have gathered thy children together, even as a hen gathereth her chickens under her wings, and ye would not!*
>
> *"Behold, your house is left unto you desolate"* (Matt. 23:37, 38).

The Jews utterly rejected God until there was nothing left. And they have suffered for their apostasy; oh, how they have suffered! Names like Dachau, Buchenwald, Treblinka, and Auschwitz stand as monuments of shame to a world gone mad under Hitler as some six million Jews were slaughtered during the Holocaust. And the awful words of the Jews ring down through the centuries as we hear them saying:

> *"His blood be on us, and on our children"* (Matt. 27:25).

Oh, how those very words have come to pass. This is a people who would long ago have been totally exterminated were it not for the awesome power of God — which has somehow kept them over the centuries. But they are coming home. There are going to be dark days ahead, but *they are coming home*.

God told Daniel:

> *"Now I am come to make thee understand what shall befall thy people in the latter days"* (Dan. 10:14).

"And there shall be a time of trouble, such as never was since there was a nation even to that same time: and at that time thy people shall be delivered, every one that shall be found written in the book" (Dan. 12:1).

This speaks of Israel. This speaks of the horror coming during the Great Tribulation period when the antichrist will make his great effort to destroy the nation of Israel.

The sad thing is that the Master prophesied that Israel would not accept *Him* as their Messiah — but another they would receive (John 5:43). "Another" is the antichrist. At the beginning of the approaching Great Tribulation period, Israel, with all her problems (surrounded by the Arab world), will find *her* saviour — the antichrist!

He will somehow convince Israel that *he* is their source of peace. *He* will be the one to appease the Arabs. The Bible says that:

"And he shall confirm the covenant with many for one week" (Dan. 9:27).

This particular *week* means a week of *years,* or seven years.

At the beginning of this period he will somehow manage to work out an agreement with the Arabs and with Israel so they can rebuild their temple on the site where the Dome of the Rock now stands.

Precisely *how* he will do this, no one knows, but *somehow* it will be worked out and Israel will rebuild her temple. They will hail the antichrist as the greatest benefactor the world has ever known, and many will actually believe he is the Messiah — the Prince of Peace.

The antichrist will do many amazing things, and tremendous feats will be accomplished.

> *"And the king shall do according to his will; and he shall exalt himself, and magnify himself above every god, and shall speak marvellous things against the God of gods, and shall prosper till the indignation be accomplished"* (Dan. 11:36).

The antichrist will worship the god of war, as is pointed out in verse 38. And then in the middle of the Great Tribulation week (in about three and one-half years) he will break his covenant, stop the sacrifice in the temple, and set up a statue of *himself* — thus causing the temple to be profaned (or an abomination, Daniel 9:27). He will then seek to completely destroy Israel, and this is when they will flee the city and seek to escape by going into the wilderness. Some think the ancient city/fortress of Petra will be their place of refuge during this period.

THE ACTUAL BATTLE

Now the stage is beginning to be set for the greatest battle ever fought in all the history of warfare. This will be a battle so unprecedented that it will change the course of history forever.

The antichrist will by now have moved his headquarters from Babylon to Jerusalem. He will desecrate the temple and break his covenant with the Jews. His desire at this point is to *annihilate* Israel, which will be his "final solution." He hates them with an irrational hatred inspired by the evil one himself, Satan. But the Bible tells us:

> *"But tidings out of the east and out of the north shall trouble him: therefore he shall go forth with great fury to destroy, and utterly to make away many"* (Dan. 11:44).

Concerning the king of the north and Soviet Russia, we might insert here that many Bible students feel that the king of the north (Dan. 11:40) is Soviet Russia. But you must remember that in the verse above we read:

> *"But tidings out of the east and out of the north shall trouble him"* (Dan. 11:44).

Of course, the "him" spoken of here is the king of the north. We must remember that there is *nothing* north of Soviet Russia. Russia is the northernmost country in the world. So the king of the north (as represented in verse 40) could *not* be the Soviet Union. Actually, it is the antichrist, out of the heart of the old Alexandrian Empire (known then as Syria but which today encompasses Syria, parts of Lebanon, Iraq, and Iran).

After the antichrist has conquered all of the countries of the old Roman Empire, the armies of Russia — allied with Japan, China, and perhaps India (the north and the east) — will trouble him. In other words, they will see him accomplishing his goal of conquering the world, and they will amass together to stop him. Of course, they won't be able to *do* this, because as he marches against them he will (with great fury) destroy them and take over their countries and their armies himself. After he has defeated these armies, they will join forces under him and march against Israel — as is recorded in Ezekiel 38 and 39 — for what is referred to as the Battle of Armageddon.

The antichrist is referred to as Gog in Ezekiel 38:2. We know this is a man, and "Gog" is actually a title given to the antichrist. We are assured he is an individual because he is called a "chief prince" and personal pronouns are used in referring to him. He is the leader of a great army that will fight at Armageddon. He is the *"little horn"* of Daniel 7:8. He is also called the *"king of the north"* in

Daniel 11; the *"man of sin,"* the *"son of perdition,"* and *"that Wicked"* in II Thessalonians 2. He is called the *"Assyrian"* in Micah 5; the *"antichrist"* in I John 2; and the *"beast"* in Revelation 13. All these Scriptures speak of a man who will come in the last days and who will make an *almost* successful bid for world domination — while simultaneously trying to annihilate Israel. He will be called Gog. And God said of him:

> *"Behold, I am against thee, O Gog, the chief prince of Meshech and Tubal"* (Ezek. 38:3).

The antichrist will gather his armies together. They will be comprised of people from many nations, including Russia, Germany, Persia, Ethiopia, Libya, and perhaps Japan, China, and India.

> *"Thou shalt ascend and come like a storm, thou shalt be like a cloud to cover the land [of Israel]"* (Ezek. 38:9).

NOT A BATTLE BETWEEN NATIONS

Many people have a misconception concerning the Battle of Armageddon. This will *not* be a battle, or a series of battles, including two sets of *earthly* opponents. It will be a battle between Christ and His heavenly armies, with earthly Israel on one side, and Satan with his angels, demons, and earthly armies under the antichrist on the other side. The antichrist will be obsessed with the desire to conquer the entire earth, *and* to destroy Israel.

Of course, the question begs to be asked, "Will the United States help Israel in that day?" There's no way to tell. The Bible doesn't say. There is some indication that *no* nation will help Israel (Zech. 14:14, 15). Of course it is *possible* that the United States will help Israel and perhaps other nations of the world, but we cannot *know* this, as the Bible does not address this point.

These will be the results of this battle:

1. The antichrist will experience total defeat and five-sixths of his great army will be destroyed (Ezek. 39:2).

2. The fowls of the air will eat of the carcasses of these armies for some seven months (Ezek. 39:4-24).

3. Blood will flow up to the horses' bridles for about 184 miles (Ezek. 39:17-24).

4. It will take some seven years to gather up the weapons for use as fuel (Ezek. 39:9).

These are indications of the sheer *magnitude* of the battle — and of the defeat the antichrist will suffer. The residue of the war will cover most of Israel and will be concentrated in the valley of Megiddo (because of its level plain) and the city of Jerusalem. This is probably the way in which it will take place:

CATACLYSMIC FINALITY
AND THE COMING OF THE LORD

The antichrist will amass his armies. They will no doubt number in the millions, perhaps even in the *tens* of millions. This will be the greatest single conflict of all time. It will be the "final solution" for a time. The "hated Jews" will now be put to death forever.

While Gog (the antichrist) cannot *personally* fight the Lord Jesus Christ (there being no way to *reach* Him), he can take out his venom and hatred upon those who brought the Messiah into this world — the Jews. As such, this will climax all the hatred of the ages directed against God's chosen people.

The Jews were persecuted by Egypt in the very beginning and by the Assyrians under Sennacherib. Next, it was the Babylonians under Nebuchadnezzar, and then the Medo-Persians under Darius and Cyrus. Then it was Alexander the Great and the Grecian Empire, followed by the mighty Roman Empire which overran Israel to become not only rulers of the pleasant land, but also of all the civilized world of the day in which Jesus was born.

After Jewry's rejection of Jesus Christ, the Jews were scattered over the face of the earth, and their nation ceased to exist until 1948 when they were driven by the Hitler persecution that attempted to annihilate them in the horror of the Holocaust.

And now here it is all over again. This is the *final* page in a long history of bloodshed and agony. At least as far as the antichrist is concerned, it *should* be the final solution. With his millions of men recruited from Russia and China, plus the revised Roman Empire, he will come down to cover the nation of Israel like a cloud of locusts.

Every major television network in the world will no doubt be represented. ABC, CBS, NBC, and others will be there to record this climactic moment of history. Through the miracle of satellite transmission, pictures of the antichrist's mighty armies could reach the homes of millions of Americans and all nations throughout the world. This great event could unfold before the eyes of the world.

The antichrist, with his mighty armies, will hit Jerusalem. You must remember, the Jews have returned from Petra (or wherever they were when the antichrist broke his covenant during the *middle* of the Great Tribulation period). They will have retaken the city while he was gone to fight his battles in the north and the east, and now they will endeavor to hold out. But he (the antichrist) will *again* appear like a cloud (Ezek. 38:9). Zechariah says this:

"For I [the Lord] will gather all nations
against Jerusalem to battle" (Zech. 14:2).

The term "all nations" does not necessarily mean *every* nation in the world, but it does mean many nations.

The world will watch raptly as Israel defends herself. This tiny country of some three million Jews has stood against approximately 100 million Arabs — and miracle after miracle has occurred as they have conspired to hold their own. But this will be the ultimate test. It will be a time of such horror that it beggars description.

The antichrist will fling his armies against all Israel, but especially against Jerusalem. It will be door-to-door fighting, house-to-house confrontations, and the city will be leveled. The Jews will have their backs to the wall. The Bible says that half the city will fall. It speaks of women being ravished and raped (Zech. 14). At that moment, with the major networks recording it for all the world to view, the Jews will realize that the die is cast. There is no further hope and all resistance is pointless. They are losing this conflict.

Despite their military superiority, it becomes obvious that they cannot win. Even if the United States were helping them (and there is no record in the Word of God that the United States will) the battle would still be in jeopardy. The antichrist is on the verge of realizing his great desire — the desire of all evil men, past and present — the final solution: total annihilation; every Jew dead; what Buchenwald, Dachau, Auschwitz, and Treblinka could not accomplish. This is what Adolf Eichmann, Adolf Hitler, and Himmler could not bring to pass. Gog will apparently accomplish it.

Realizing there is no longer hope, and as a pall of smoke hangs over the city and flames leap from house to house, the roar of artillery and the scream of jets echo over Jerusalem. The city of peace has once more been turned into a city of blood. It looks like Dante's inferno — a veritable hell on earth. The antichrist spurs his armies to push even harder. Victory is in sight and nothing can stop them. The hated Jews will be annihilated once and for all. This despised Messiah called Jesus Christ will be eliminated from the face of the earth. Gog will become god instead of the God of the heavens and His beloved Christ. The hated Jews who are linked with the Messiah will be exterminated forever. Once that is brought about, Gog will be the prince of the earth and god of the mighty.

David Ben-Gurion, before he died, was asked, "What is Israel's future — what is Israel's hope?" This man, with white locks bespeaking the wisdom of years, looked down toward the ground and finally said, with a faraway look in his eyes, "The hope of Israel is the coming of the Messiah."

The Jews will know that the battle is lost and there is no hope. No one will come to their rescue. The United States either cannot or *will* not help in this hour. Other nations of the world will stand back, fearing the wrath of mighty Gog. It is *then* they will begin to cry. It is then they will weep as never before for the Messiah to come. There will be a sudden cry that will fill the city in the midst of the din — the scream of cannon shells, mortar bursts, and machine-gun fire. They will wail like babies screaming in pain. They will beg; they will plead. They will *cry* for the Messiah to come.

In Ezekiel, God said:

> *"And it shall come to pass at the same time when Gog shall come against the land of Israel, saith the Lord God, that my fury shall come up in my face.*
> *"For in my jealousy and in the fire of my wrath have I spoken"* (Ezek. 38:18, 19).

*"Then shall the Lord go forth, and fight
against those nations, as when he fought in the
day of battle"* (Zech. 14:3).

As the television cameras record this appalling series
of events, something shall transpire that has never before
been seen nor ever shall be seen again.

Just when it seems that the antichrist has overcome
Israel and all hope is gone — with half of Jerusalem fallen
and the rest expected to fall at any moment — the television
announcer will be struck *tongue-tied* as he tries to comprehend what is occurring. No one will understand. Suddenly
the cameras will pan *upward* as announcers attempt to
instruct the waiting world on events *they* don't understand.

Oh, can't you see it? In millions of homes throughout
the world, people will be frozen in attention. The sky will
be literally *filled*, rank upon rank, troop upon troop, and
regiment upon regiment, with the heavenly host of the
Lord Jesus Christ.

This is the Lord Jesus Christ; and every saint who has
ever lived will be there — riding upon white horses as they
come back to fight (as in the days of old). And when this
happens, the sky will radiate an eerie, diffused light. The
battle will last one day (which shall be known to the Lord
as neither day nor night), but it shall come to pass that at
evening time it shall be light (Zech. 14:7). In other words,
the light will change. It will be partly dark during the day
and partly light during the night.

John recorded it:

*"And I saw heaven opened, and behold a
white horse; and he that sat upon him was called
Faithful and True, and in righteousness he doth
judge and make war.*

"His eyes were as a flame of fire, and on his

*head were many crowns; and he had a name
written, that no man knew, but he himself.*

*"And he was clothed with a vesture dipped in
blood: and his name is called The Word of God.*

*"And the armies which were in heaven fol-
lowed him upon white horses, clothed in fine
linen, white and clean.*

*"And out of his mouth goeth a sharp sword,
that with it he should smite the nations: and he
shall rule them with a rod of iron: and he
treadeth the winepress of the fierceness and
wrath of Almighty God.*

*"And he hath on his vesture and on his thigh
a name written, KING OF KINGS, AND LORD
OF LORDS"* (Rev. 19:11-16).

In Ezekiel 38:22, God said He would pour out
pestilence with blood upon the antichrist. He would rain
upon him and upon his bands an overflowing rain and great
hailstones, fire, and brimstone. God said,

*"And I will smite thy bow out of thy left hand,
and will cause thine arrows to fall out of thy right
hand.*

*"Thou shalt fall upon the mountains of
Israel, thou, and all thy bands, and the people
that is with thee: I will give thee unto the ravenous birds of every sort, and to the beasts of the
field to be devoured.*

*"Thou shalt fall upon the open field: for I
have spoken it, saith the Lord God"* (Ezek.
39:3-5).

At the time of this monumental event — the Second
Coming — the Bible tells us:

"And his feet shall stand in that day upon the mount of Olives, which is before Jerusalem on the east, and the mount of Olives shall cleave in the midst thereof toward the east and toward the west, and there shall be a very great valley" (Zech. 14:4).

In this terrible conflict the blood shall run to the horses' bridles for miles about — many men will die, requiring seven months for their burial — and Israel will in that hour be *victorious*. Jesus Christ will return. The antichrist will be killed and cast into the lake of fire.

Satan will be bound, and this will climax the Battle of Armageddon. Israel will suffer losses, to be sure, but the heavenly army will suffer *no* losses. The *bulk* of the casualties will be suffered by the antichrist and *his* armies.

All this will usher in the great kingdom called the Millennial Age — where Jesus Christ will set up His kingdom to reign a thousand years. Then:

"The desert shall rejoice, and blossom as the rose" (Isa. 35:1).

"The earth shall be full of the knowledge of the Lord, as the waters cover the sea" (Isa. 11:9).

"Even so, come, Lord Jesus" (Rev. 22:20).

CHAPTER 10

WHAT IS THE MILLENNIAL REIGN? WILL IT BE A LITERAL KINGDOM? EXACTLY WHAT WILL IT BE LIKE?

The word "millennium," of which millennial is a form, is not found in the Bible, but it simply means "one thousand years" — and that term is repeated some six times in Revelation 20:1-7.

The thousand-year millennial reign will start when Jesus Christ comes back with all of the saints, interrupting the Battle of Armageddon, and sets His feet upon the Mount of Olivet and sets up His kingdom in Jerusalem. At that moment the millennial reign will begin.

We know that Satan must first be bound (Rev. 20:1-10), for we read in Revelation 20:3 that Satan will be bound during the millennium. Also, Revelation 20:5 tells us that the tribulation martyrs will have a part in the first resurrection, which takes place before the thousand years and includes all the different companies of the redeemed and every individual saved — from Adam to the binding of Satan. This verse also implies that the tribulation saints will be the last redeemed company resurrected and translated. The first resurrection ends with the rapture of this company and the two witnesses.

It will be a literal kingdom, with Jesus Christ reigning in Jerusalem — and in the following statements we will prove this from the Word of God and give some particulars as to exactly what it will be like.

First of all, the millennial reign is called several different things. I will not attempt to give all the Scriptures, to conserve space, but I will give some of the names it's referred to in the Word of God.

- The thousand-year reign of Christ
- The dispensation of the fullness of time
- The day of the Lord
- That day
- The age to come
- The kingdom of Christ and of God
- The kingdom of God
- The kingdom of heaven
- The regeneration
- The times of the restoration of all things
- The consolation of Israel
- The redemption of Jerusalem

I think this pretty well covers the various different names given to this beautiful age that is yet to come and will so begin.

THE LENGTH OF THE MILLENNIAL REIGN

As already stated, in Revelation 20:1-7, the expression "thousand years" is mentioned six times in these Scriptures. So we know from this that the millennial reign will last until the loosing of Satan, the last rebellion, the renovation of the earth by fire, and the Great White Throne Judgment (Rev. 20:11-15; II Pet. 3:8-13).

Man will have a beginning more favorable at this time than in any other dispensation: the God of heaven for a ruler and all the privileges that such rulership will bring.

WHEN WILL THE KINGDOM BE SET UP?

• At the return of the King from glory (Matt. 25:31-46; Isa. 9:6, 7; Dan. 2:44, 45).

• After the church is raptured (I Cor. 15:51-58; I Thes. 4:13-17).

• The church will come back with Christ to help Him set up the kingdom and reign over the nations (Zech. 14:1-5; Jude 14; Rev. 1:4, 5). We know from II Thessalonians 2:7, 8 that the church is raptured before the revelation of the antichrist, and the antichrist will be revealed before Christ comes (II Thes. 2:1-6). So the kingdom cannot be set up until after these events take place.

• After the future tribulation, then, the Lord will come to the earth with the saints (Matt. 24:15-31; Zech. 14:1-21; Dan. 12:1-13; Rev. 19:11-21).

• The antichrist will be destroyed at Christ's coming, so he must be here when the Lord comes (II Thes. 2:1-12; Rev. 19:11-21; Dan. 7:18-27).

• At the time the antichrist is destroyed, Satan will be bound for a thousand years (Rev. 20:2, 7). Christ will reign on the earth during that time. Realizing that Satan will be bound during that thousand years and knowing that he is now loose, we know we are still living in the Church Age and will be until Christ comes to bind the devil, at which time we will enter into the great millennial reign.

• The kingdom will be set up when Ezekiel's temple is built, which will be on the site where Solomon's temple sat, as is recorded in Ezekiel 41-43.

A LITERAL EARTHLY KINGDOM

This confuses a lot of people — but as all preceding kingdoms have been literal, so this one will be literal as well (Isa. 9:6, 7; Dan. 2:44, 45; 7:13; Zech. 14; Rev. 17:8-18).

THE FORM OF GOVERNMENT

It will not be monarchic, democratic, or autocratic, but it will be a theocratic form of government — which simply means God will reign through the Lord Jesus Christ (Matt. 25:31-46; Luke 1:32-35; Rev. 11:15) *and* through David, who will actually rule the nation of Israel (Jer. 30:9; Ezek. 34:24; Hos. 3:4, 5).

God will also rule through the apostles and all saints from Adam to the millennium. All saints that have ever lived will be judged and rewarded according to the deeds done in the body, and will be given places of rulership according to their rewards — not according to the company of redeemed of which they are a part or the age in which they were redeemed or lived.

To give you an example, David will have a greater rulership than any one of the apostles. He is to be king over all Israel unto Christ, while the apostles will have only one tribe each. For instance, some of the Old Testament saints did much more for God and had more power than the average New Testament saint, and they will be given authority commensurate with that which they did while on this earth (I Cor. 4:8; Eph. 2:7; II Tim. 2:12; Rom. 8:17; II Thes. 1:4-7; Psa. 149:5-9).

Jerusalem will be rebuilt and restored to a greater glory than ever before and it will be the seat of government, the world capital, and the center of worship forever (I Chr. 23:25; Psa. 48:8; Isa. 2:2-4; Jer. 17:25; Joel 3:17-20; Zech. 8:3-23).

The millennial kingdom will be worldwide and will forever increase in every respect just as every other kingdom — except that it will not have sin and rebellion (Isa. 9:6, 7; Psa. 72:8; Dan. 7:13, 14; Zech. 9:10; Rev. 11:15).

All nations now in existence on the earth, and who will be living when Christ comes, will continue as such in the kingdom forever and ever. All people, nations, and languages shall serve Him. His dominion is an everlasting dominion which shall not pass away, and His kingdom shall not be destroyed.

After the Battle of Armageddon and the Judgment of the Nations at the return of Christ, there will be many of all nations left who will go up from year to year to worship the Lord of Hosts and keep the Feast of Tabernacles (Zech. 14:16-21; Matt. 25:31-46; Rev. 11:15).

LAWS OF THE KINGDOM

There will be laws in this kingdom, and it will be for the same purpose as in any other kingdom. The kingdom will be a literal, earthly one with earthly subjects, many of whom, sad to say, will be rebels in heart against the rule of Christ and will openly rebel at the first chance they get when the devil is loosed out of the pit at the end of the thousand years (Rev. 20:1-10). However, *anyone* truly born again and baptized in the Holy Spirit, and who enjoyed fellowship with God during the thousand years, certainly will not rebel with Satan at that time.

That there will be sinners here during the millennium is clear from Isaiah 2:2-4; Micah 4:3; and Zechariah 14:16-21.

Many unsaved people will be permitted to live and go through the millennium because of keeping the outward laws of the government, but, sad to say, in their hearts they will be rebellious against the government. On the other hand, some will be executed during the millennium because of committing sins worthy of death (Isa. 11:3-5; 16:5; 65:20).

The laws of God revealing His will in detail, as given by Moses and Jesus Christ, will be the laws of the kingdom. This will include the laws of both the Old and the New Testaments. It would seem from Isaiah, Micah, and Ezekiel that the law of Moses will again become effective during the millennium and forever (Isa. 2:2-4; Mic. 4:2; Ezek. 40:1; 48:35). And of course, as stated, the laws of Jesus Christ as laid down in the four gospels will also be paramount; neither will conflict with the other.

Christ and the glorified saints who have been made kings and priests will execute these laws forever.

LOCATIONS OF THE DIFFERENT NATIONS

The Gentile nations will perhaps live in the same place as they do today, with the exception of those who live in the lands promised to Abraham and his seed (Israel) for an everlasting procession. The Promised Land, as given by God, was from the Mediterranean Sea on the west to the River Euphrates on the east, taking in all the Arabian Peninsula and possibly Syria as well, and including the wilderness countries south and east of Palestine. So it would seem that all the nations of the world would basically remain exactly as they are, with some minor exceptions, understanding that Israel will incorporate that which God promised in the beginning and was really never fully realized. Consequently, some parts of the nations of Syria, Lebanon, Jordan, and Saudi Arabia possibly might be eliminated (Gen. 15:14-18; Exo. 32:13; Deut. 4:40; Josh. 14:2-9; Ezek. 47:13-23).

The Jews will have a temple during the millennial reign. It will be located at the site where Solomon, Zerubbabel, and Herod built their temples — all of which were on the same site. However, it must be understood that this temple will not be the one that will be built in the last days before the Second Coming of Christ — the one in which the antichrist will sit during the last three and one-half years of the Tribulation period. The millennial temple will be built by Christ Himself when He comes to the earth to set up His kingdom (Zech. 6:12, 13). It will be the place for Christ's earthly throne forever (Ezek. 43:7).

THE RIVER OF THE MILLENNIAL TEMPLE

There will be a literal river flowing out from this temple eastward and from the south side of the altar (in Jerusalem). Half of it will flow into the Dead Sea and half into the Mediterranean. The Dead Sea will be healed so that multitudes of fish will be found in it (Ezek. 47:1-12; Zech. 14:8). Actually, when the Lord comes back and sets His feet on the Mount of Olives with all the saints, there will be a great earthquake and the whole country will be changed (Zech. 14:4, 5). The Dead Sea will be raised so that it will have an outlet to purify the stagnant waters which have been shut up for all these centuries. There will also be trees on both sides of the river whose leaves shall not fade, neither shall the fruit be consumed. The trees shall bring forth new fruit according to their months, which shall be for meat and preservation of natural life for the nations. It could be that these trees will be similar to the Tree of Life that existed in the Garden of Eden.

THE SPIRITUAL CONDITION

In Joel 2:28-32, we are told that the Holy Spirit will be poured out as never before in the millennial reign. God's promises to this world, even with the salvation of millions and the infilling of the Holy Spirit by the millions, have really not been realized as of yet and will not be realized until the great millennial reign. Then, multiple hundreds of millions will be saved by the blood of Jesus Christ — exactly as they are today. Then, millions will be baptized in the Holy Spirit according to Acts 2:4 — exactly as they are today. In other words, that which was received by the early church is being received today and will be received in a greater way throughout all eternity from the time the Messiah comes to bring universal peace and prosperity to all. But what you must understand, this only includes the *natural* people who are on the earth. All the saints of God who have lived from the time of Adam to the millennium will have glorified bodies and will, of course, not need to be saved because they already will have been saved.

UNIVERSAL KNOWLEDGE

Universal knowledge (outlined in Isa. 11:9; Hab. 2:14; Zech. 8:22, 23) actually means that all people will know of the ways of the Lord. There will not be people ignorant of His ways as they are today. Sad to say, most of the people on this planet today do not know of the ways of the Lord, but then there will be universal knowledge and all will know of His ways.

JEWISH MISSIONARIES

The term "Jewish missionaries" sounds somewhat strange, but actually that's what will happen. The Jewish people will become the missionaries of the gospel and the priests of the law during this age and forever. Of course they will be aided and abetted by the glorified saints and others, but it will be they who will primarily serve in the capacity of missionaries because they will be natural people in a natural setting (Isa. 2:2-4; Zech. 8:23; Isa. 52:7; Isa. 66:18-21).

It will become popular then to serve God and the Lord Jesus Christ. There won't be all different types of faiths and religions; there will be only one and that will be the religion of the Lord Jesus Christ, or it could better be said the salvation of the Lord Jesus Christ (Mal. 1:11; Zech. 14:6-21; Isa. 2:2-4; Joel 2:28-31; Jer. 31:31-36). All the teachings of the Lord, of course, will be based on the Word of God.

LIVING CONDITIONS

Satan will be bound. There will be no tempter (Rev. 20:1-10; Isa. 24:21).

There will be universal peace. This means there will be no taxation to keep up large armies and navies. The universal conversation will not be about war, treaties, armament, depression, varied religions and forms of government, but people will be fully satisfied in peace and prosperity and will have no excuse to talk about anything but the goodness and greatness of God and the wonder of His reign (Mal. 1:11; Isa. 2:4; 9:6, 7; Mic. 4:3, 4).

There will be universal prosperity. We are told this in Isaiah 65:24 and Micah 4:4, 5. All investments will be safe. Everybody will have their needs met. There will be no financial crises to retire businesses throughout eternity. The God of all will prosper all people and any legitimate businesses. All people will be capable of succeeding in life and having a life of prosperity. All poverty will be abolished.

Tithing will be the financial system. Tithing was the system before the Law, it was the system under the Law, and it has been the system since the Law. So no doubt the same system will be used by the government of Christ in the coming ages. There will be plenty of money from such a system to balance the budget and have plenty to spare. There will be no corrupt politics or graft, as Christ and the glorified saints will reign in righteousness and true holiness (Isa. 32:1-5).

There will be full justice for all. Crime waves will be a thing of the past. The Lord and His glorified saints will try and judge all men, thus assuring justice to all alike. If a man commits a sin worthy of death, he will be immediately tried and executed. There will not be a thousand ways of staying execution or prolonging trial. The law will be enforced to the letter, as it should be under man today (Isa. 9:6, 7; 11:3-5; 65:20; Matt. 5:7).

Human life will be prolonged. Human life will be prolonged to a thousand years, and then those who do not rebel against God with Satan at the end of the millennium will be permitted to live on forever and ever (Isa. 65:20; Zech. 8:4; Luke 1:33).

There will be an increase of light. Notice that it says an increase of light and not an increase of heat. The light of the sun will be increased seven times and the light of the moon will be as the light of the sun today. No doubt there will be a healing feature in this increased light (Isa. 30:26; 60:18-22).

There will be changes in the animal kingdom. All animals will have their natures changed. There will be none that will be fierce or poisonous. Things will be as they were in the Garden of Eden before the curse, with the exception of the serpent who still will be cursed (Isa. 11:6-8; Gen. 3:14; Isa. 65:25).

There will be a great restoration. All lands will be restored to a wonderful beauty and fruitfulness with the exception of the site of Babylon and perhaps a few more centers of great rebellion against God, which will be used as object lessons to coming generations of God's wrath on sin. The ugliness and blight that characterizes so much of the world today because of sin and rebellion against God will be done away with and the great restoration will take place (Isa. 35; Jer. 50, 51).

Love and righteousness will prevail. The Gentiles will love the Jews and the Jews will love the Gentiles, and there will be no more animosity, hatred, or jealousy among the races.

WHAT IS GOD'S PURPOSE
IN DOING ALL OF THIS?

• To put down all rebellion and all enemies under the feet of Christ so that God may be all and all as before the rebellion (I Cor. 15:24-28; Heb. 2:7-9; Eph. 1:10).

• To fulfill the everlasting covenants He made with Abraham (Gen. 12, 26, 28, 35; II Sam. 7).

• To vindicate and avenge Christ and His saints (Matt. 26:63-66; Rom. 12:19; I Pet. 1:10, 11).

• To restore Israel and deliver them from the nations and make them the head of all nations forever (Acts 15:13-17; Matt. 24:31; Isa. 11:11; Deut. 28).

• To exalt the saints of all ages in some kingly or priestly capacity according to the promises and according to their works (Rom. 8:17-21; II Cor. 5:10; Phil. 3:20; Col. 3:4; Rev. 1:5).

• To gather together in "one" all things in Christ which are in heaven and in earth and restore all things as before the rebellion (Eph. 1:10; Acts 3:21; I Cor. 15:24-28).

• To judge the nations in righteousness and restore the earth to its rightful owners (Isa. 2:2-4; Matt. 25:31-46; Dan. 7:9-27; I Cor. 6).

• To restore a righteous and eternal government on earth as originally planned (Isa. 9:6, 7; Dan. 2:44, 45; Luke 1:32-35; Rev. 11:15; 22:5).

The millennial reign will be the greatest age to date the world has ever known. Jesus Christ will personally reign supreme from Jerusalem. David will reign over all of Israel under the Lord Jesus Christ. Every saint that's ever lived from the time of Adam to the millennium will be here in glorified bodies. The world will then know what it actually could have had all of these thousands of years that it lived in rebellion against God. It will then know the peace and prosperity that God intended from the very beginning. The only way to enter into this great kingdom that's coming is by accepting the Lord Jesus Christ as your own personal Saviour (Rom. 10:9, 10; John 3:16).

11

THE FUTURE OF PLANET EARTH

If we were to seek out a single word to describe the general mood of the public today, the most accurate and all-encompassing might well be "fear." Why should fear be a widespread and all-pervasive burden during these "enlightened" days of technological advancement and drudgery-free automation? Because the average citizen senses that the clock is rapidly running down, and that the period of opportunity might well be drawing to a close. The doomsday "second hand" would appear to be on its final circuit and sweeping rapidly upward toward the stroke of twelve.

Anyone living in the world cannot be blamed for having a pessimistic attitude. The news floods us daily with fresh announcements of a rapidly expanding storehouse of mysterious weapons capable of leaving the earth completely unlivable in one fatal stroke. Neutron bombs, laser space weapons, radar-masking aircraft, and "first-strike vulnerability" fill the airwaves as the average viewer gnaws his fingernails down to the quick. One famous scientist even made the statement that it is conceivable that the explosion of *one single weapon* could effectively destroy the earth.

The question must of course be asked: Would anyone be foolish enough to *start* an all-out atomic confrontation? To answer that question, we might look back into history. Not long before Albert Speer died, he was asked: If Hitler had commanded an atomic arsenal as World War II ground to a close, would he have used it?

Speer, Hitler's supply minister, took only a moment to consider the question. "Yes," he answered, "Hitler *would* have detonated the bomb." This, coupled with the historical fact of Truman's approval of the atomic annihilation of Hiroshima and Nagasaki, would certainly lead one to the conclusion that atomic warfare is by no means "unthinkable" under the pressures and urgencies of all-out warfare.

Add to this the fact that any number of Middle East countries — many commanded by *unstable* dictators, monarchs, or politicians — have now, or soon will have, an atomic capability. A "local" atomic shootout would no doubt rapidly involve the super powers, rushing headlong into World War III. That fact is hardly reassuring. The Israeli destruction of the Iraqi atomic plant and the subsequent bombing of Beirut, Lebanon, point up the extreme explosiveness of the Middle East.

And, of course, the prospect of nuclear, bacteriological, or chemical annihilation is not the *only* doomsday picture hanging over our heads. Social scientists tell us that the world is now hard-pressed to feed the 5 billion people *now* populating its surface.

And the future?

They say that this already unmanageable number will *surely* expand to 15 or 18 billion by the year 2000, and *perhaps* to as many as 25 or 30 billion.

Incredible? Well, don't worry about that. Still *other* scientists tell us we are running out of fuel while a new Ice Age is creeping up just over the horizon; *unless* still other scientists are correct and the increase of carbon dioxide in the atmosphere causes a "greenhouse" effect — cooking us all like a mess of crawfish in a pot on the stove.

Haven't heard enough?

Well, what about the environmentalists who predict that within a few years we will all go out "not with a bang but with a whimper," as we succumb to the accumulated effects of pollution plus nuclear and hazardous wastes? They delight in mournfully describing to us collections of debris and garbage floating thousands of miles at sea — and the so-called "acid rain" which affects wilderness vegetation and streams half a continent away from their sources.

What *is* the future of Planet Earth? What *is* going to happen? Will we be destroyed in the mushroom cloud of atomic warfare? Will we strangle in our own mire of pollution? Will the earth freeze into immobility or bake like a giant meringue? Wouldn't it be nice to *know* what is going to happen?

THIS IS WHAT IS GOING TO HAPPEN.

There is certainly a broad spectrum of unpleasant alternatives open to anyone who chooses to meditate upon the eventual demise (extinction) of mankind. But try as they might, scientists are not going to come up with a *rational* appraisal of mankind's chances until they turn to the *ultimate* scientific discipline — by opening their Bibles.

The Bible? In this day of scientific enlightenment? Well, let's put things into perspective. Science can be defined in one short phrase — "a search for truth." While this implies *true* science — and not some of the perverted

and distorted farces *masquerading* as science today —
there is only *one* place to find the *true* prospect for the
world and its peoples, and that is within the covers of the
Word of God!

First of all, the Bible says that God made the earth.

> *"He hath made the earth by his power,*
> *he hath established the world by his wisdom,*
> *and hath stretched out the heaven by his under-*
> *standing"* (Jer. 51:15).

Earlier, in Genesis it tells us:

> *"In the beginning God created the heaven*
> *and the earth"* (Gen. 1:1).

So *He* is the builder, developer, and ultimately the
owner of this planet. David said in the Psalms:

> *"The earth is the Lord's, and the fulness*
> *thereof; the world, and they that dwell therein"*
> (Psa. 24:1).

So we know that the earth belongs to the Lord, and that
He did not *make* the earth only to allow it to be destroyed by
Satan. Satan, of course, is the *author* of pestilence, "ice
ages," and even the proposed increase of the sun's rays to
where they will burn the world to a crisp.

John tells us of the contradictory motives of Satan and
Jesus Christ:

> *"The thief cometh not, but for to steal, and*
> *to kill, and to destroy"* (John 10:10).

Our Lord and Saviour, on the other hand, promises:

"I am come that they might have life, and that they might have it more abundantly" (John 10:10).

So all the problems we see in this world are caused by Satan, while *none* are caused by God. And God still has plans for this planet. He has clearly outlined them within His Word and this is what we have to look forward to:

THE RAPTURE

"For the Lord himself shall descend from heaven with a shout, with the voice of the archangel, and with the trump of God: and the dead in Christ shall rise first:

"Then we which are alive and remain shall be caught up together with them in the clouds, to meet the Lord in the air: and so shall we ever be with the Lord" (I Thes. 4:16, 17).

So the next great event on the horizon of time (perhaps the greatest in all of history) is the rapture. Of course the specific word "rapture" is not *found* in the Bible, but basically it means "ecstatic joy" and also "a catching away." There is going to be (because it is described in Scripture) a "snatching away," and I think we can be assured that this *will* be — for the participants — a time of unparalleled joy.

This is the beginning of the "first resurrection," the resurrection of life. This is the time when every child of God who has ever lived — all the way from Adam until the trump of God sounds — will be "instantly changed" in the "twinkling of an eye."

The Bible assures us that corruption will put on incorruption, and mortality will put on immortality. The soul and the spirit of every Christian who has ever lived will then be reunited with their deceased bodies. Their bodies will be resurrected and simultaneously changed as they reunite with their souls and spirits in heaven.

We call this the "rapture" and it is the next great event on the horizon. It's going to be the most shattering event to ever take place in all of human history. What better way to get the attention of mankind than to instantly withdraw *millions* of people from the face of the earth?

That's what is going to happen and that's what we're looking forward to *at this moment*. It is, without question, the next great spiritual event to erupt onto the stage of history.

And how does one come to be *included* in this joyful assemblage rising to meet the Lord Jesus Christ in the air? The only requirement for participating in the rapture is to be saved by the blood of the Lamb. Joining a particular church will not suffice. Accepting the doctrines of a specific denomination will not do. Trusting in any *church* to save you will prove an insurmountable obstacle, as the only condition for inclusion is salvation through the blood of Jesus.

And, of course, to "be saved" means to follow the Lord with all your heart — and with all of your life — and to do your very best to serve Him as this better way is revealed to you.

THE GREAT TRIBULATION

"For then shall be great tribulation, such as was not since the beginning of the world to this time, no, nor ever shall be" (Matt. 24:21).

This is, of course, the "Great Tribulation" period of which Jesus spoke — and which is to last for seven years.

The first three and one-half years will be a period of trials and heartaches as the antichrist bursts onto the world's stage. The *last* three and one-half years will be so horrifying that the minds of men will scarcely comprehend. They will even pray to die.

The book of Revelation gives us graphic descriptions of the seals, the trumpets, the four horsemen of the apocalypse, and all the other awesome consequences to befall the earth at this time.

Once again we must emphasize the words of Jesus. He called it *"a great tribulation."* He said, even with all the problems mankind had already experienced, that no one could imagine the frightful scourges that would be inflicted upon mankind in this day. Nor, once past, would such a period ever again be known.

Basically, the Great Tribulation period is to occur for two reasons: First, it is to *punish* the world for iniquity, to finally punish the world for its sin. As so many Christians have asked over the years, "Why doesn't God put an end to this filth and perversion by *punishing* sin and wrong?"

At this time, that's exactly what will happen. God will finally "take off the gloves." It will be a time of unimaginable suffering — a time when God will pour out His judgments upon a planet that has forsaken Him for days without number.

And secondly, the Great Tribulation is to bring Israel to the Lord Jesus Christ. This is also referred to in Scripture as *"the time of Jacob's trouble."* The primary subject of the Tribulation (and also of the book of Revelation) is Israel. Israel has seen dark days in the past, but she will see even darker days during the Great Tribulation period because she has refused to collectively bend her knees to her Messiah. Even though *all* people on this planet will be affected by the Great Tribulation period, the nation of Israel will be affected most of all.

To begin with, they will have mistakenly accepted the "beast" (of Revelation and Daniel) as the Messiah. They will accept him wholeheartedly, and only when it is too late will they realize that they have been deceived. He will desecrate the holy temple that will, at this time, be rebuilt.

Many of the Jews will flee Jerusalem and go to the ancient city of Petra where they will be protected by God. Were it not for the direct intervention of God, the antichrist's armies would follow them and they would be completely annihilated.

But God will intervene and they will be saved — when the antichrist goes northward and eastward to put down a rebellion and take still more countries. Much of this remnant (from Petra) will then return to Jerusalem where, during the Battle of Armageddon, they will once again be assailed.

Then, as Zechariah said, half the city will fall as they come under tremendous pressure. They will then cry as they never have before for the Messiah to return. That's when Jesus Christ will come.

THE COMING OF THE LORD

"And I saw heaven opened, and behold a white horse; and he that sat upon him was called Faithful and True, and in righteousness he doth judge and make war.

"His eyes were as a flame of fire, and on his head were many crowns; and he had a name written, that no man knew, but he himself.

"And he was clothed with a vesture dipped in blood: and his name is called The Word of God.

"And the armies which were in heaven followed him upon white horses, clothed in fine linen, white and clean.

"And out of his mouth goeth a sharp sword, that with it he should smite the nations: and he shall rule them with a rod of iron: and he treadeth the winepress of the fierceness and wrath of Almighty God.

"And he hath on his vesture and on his thigh a name written, KING OF KINGS, AND LORD OF LORDS" (Rev. 19:11-16).

"And then shall appear the sign of the Son of man in heaven: and then shall all the tribes of the earth mourn, and they shall see the Son of man coming in the clouds of heaven with power and great glory" (Matt. 24:30).

This is called the "Second Coming of the Lord," which is totally different from the rapture. At the time of the rapture, the Lord will come *for* His saints. At the Second Coming, He will come *with* His saints.

At the rapture, the Lord will not touch this earth; He will come only part-way *between* heaven and earth. At the Second Coming, He will actually set His feet upon the Mount of Olivet (Zech. 14:4).

The Jews will then accept the Lord Jesus Christ (Zech. 12:7-10). His coming will start a new era, an era of greatness and glory. The Lord will judge the nations, and all the former difficulties and woes — to which we have been heirs ever since the fall of Adam — will fade from memory. All human perversions — war, murder, crime, poverty, heartache, and despair — will be totally banished. Such will be the state of Planet Earth during the millennial reign.

THE THOUSAND-YEAR REIGN OF CHRIST

"And I saw an angel come down from heaven, having the key of the bottomless pit and

a great chain in his hand.

"And he laid hold on the dragon, that old serpent, which is the Devil, and Satan, and bound him a thousand years,

"And cast him into the bottomless pit, and shut him up, and set a seal upon him, that he should deceive the nations no more, till the thousand years should be fulfilled: and after that he must be loosed a little season.

". . . and they lived and reigned with Christ a thousand years" (Rev. 20:1-4).

The word "millenia" is a Latin word meaning "thousand." Like the word "rapture," it cannot be found in the Bible. But this is the word that has come to be used in describing the thousand-year reign of Christ. This is to be a literal kingdom — the kingdom of God on earth — *"Thy kingdom come."* This is not some symbolic concept one can apply to his personal life as some teach today. It is the literal and tangible kingdom of Jesus Christ reigning on earth from the city of Jerusalem (Zech. 14:17).

Finally, the world will come to know the *original* plan of God in its fullness. God intended from the beginning that the world would be a veritable paradise — free of all the difficulties assailing us today. What thwarted God's original plan? Of course, Adam and Eve fell. *When* Adam and Eve fell, they changed lords! God was no longer their lord; Satan became lord of the earth. We've been partakers of the consequences of their fall ever since.

During Christ's thousand-year millennial reign, of course, Satan will be locked away in the bottomless pit. At this time he will not be *"going to and fro in the earth. . . walking up and down in it"* as described in Job 2:2. For a thousand years Satan's sinful influence will be completely absent from the earth.

All the difficulties man has experienced throughout the corridors of time will disappear. All poverty, sickness, sorrow, and heartache will be eliminated. The Bible states:

> *"And they shall beat their swords into plowshares, and their spears into pruning-hooks: nation shall not lift up sword against nation, neither shall they learn war any more"* (Isa. 2:4).

Obviously, war will be eliminated. As we look at the problems in the world today — grinding poverty with millions going to bed hungry each night — think of the marvelous new age beckoning unto us. Think of the *hundreds of billions* of dollars being spent today on armaments and weapons, whose only reason for existence is *destruction*. The monies spent on weapons could almost instantaneously solve the problems of poverty throughout the world.

Then there will be no war and no *reason* to manufacture weapons of war. All the money, sweat, and toil now going into producing arms can be used to produce implements for farming and industry — thus assisting mankind rather than destroying it:

> *"And they shall build houses, and inhabit them; and they shall plant vineyards, and eat the fruit of them"* (Isa. 65:21).

God also tells us:

> *"Of the increase of his government and peace there shall be no end, upon the throne of David, and upon his kingdom, to order it, and to*

establish it with judgment and with justice from henceforth even for ever. The zeal of the Lord of hosts will perform this" (Isa. 9:7).

What a statement this is! *Today,* even when things seem to be going well for a time, we are still beset by the pressures and uncertainties of the perilous times in which we live. Even though it's okay right now, how long can it last? How long before a new development makes our jobs obsolete? How long before some power-crazed dictator lights the fuse of world consumption?

Ah, but the millennium! Once Christ's reign of peace, certainty, and assurance begins, we will know that there will never be an end to it. Men will no longer have to face with dread the coming of a future beset by peril, fear, and potential annihilation. No more worries about politicians with their fingers poised above the panic button. No more antacids to "get us through the day." All this will be consigned eternally to the past. *"Of the increase of his government and peace there shall be no end."* Praise the Lord!

We are also told:

"The wolf also shall dwell with the lamb, and the leopard shall lie down with the kid; and the calf and the young lion and the fatling together; and a little child shall lead them.

"And the cow and the bear shall feed; their young ones shall lie down together: and the lion shall eat straw like the ox.

"And the sucking child shall play on the hole of the asp, and the weaned child shall put his hand on the cockatrice' den." (Isa. 11:6-8).

This is a revelation of awesome dimension. The whole *spirit* of the world will be changed. No longer will the ravenous animal spirit permeate all of mankind (and, of course, the animal kingdom).The Bible refers specifically to the animal kingdom and how it will revert back to the nature that prevailed before the fall.

But how much more the attitudes of *man*. It is basically the influence of Satan that instills the dog-eat-dog attitude in the world today. Man was never intended to compete so fiercely, to seek only his own goals — to the detriment of his brothers.

But what do we have today? We have an economy encouraging and promoting "breaking the other guy" as we climb on *his* shoulders to *our* pinnacle. And all this in an environment created by God and supplied with more than enough resources — if only we would share them in brotherhood and love. This spirit — authored by Satan — will be absent from Planet Earth as the devil stews in solitude in the bottomless pit.

The Bible speaks of the wolf and the lamb dwelling in harmony, and of the child playing on the hole of the serpent without suffering any ill effects. How do you sum it up? Isaiah already did:

> "They shall not hurt nor destroy in all my
> holy mountain: for the earth shall be full of the
> knowledge of the Lord, as the waters cover the
> sea" (Isa. 11:9).

So we will be totally rid of the "natural" tendency to hurt and destroy. The attitude of mankind of "What's in it for me?" will be eternally abolished and removed from our memories. Love will be the order of the day; peace will rule.

There will be an entirely different attitude and atmosphere. The "rat-race" of today will no longer exist. "Get-him-before-he-gets-you" will no longer be the rule of the day. The Beatitudes will *finally* become the law of the land as Jesus Christ reigns in all His glory.

The Bible also tells us:

> *"And he will destroy in this mountain the face of the covering cast over all people, and the vail that is spread over all nations.*
>
> *"He will swallow up death in victory; and the Lord God will wipe away tears from off all faces; and the rebuke of his people shall he take away from off all the earth: for the Lord hath spoken it"* (Isa. 25:7, 8).

The satanic curse will finally be removed from off the earth. The land will give forth an abundance of crops. The Scripture speaks of the desert blooming as the rose. Zechariah describes it:

> *"For the seed shall be prosperous; the vine shall give her fruit, and the ground shall give her increase, and the heavens shall give their dew; and I will cause the remnant of this people to possess all these things"* (Zech. 8:12).

The earth will no longer yield thorns and thistles, but crops in such abundance that the population of the world will live in plenty. Nations will no longer wage war on one another, but will work together in cooperation under the Lord Jesus Christ.

And, thank God, death will no longer be the fearful pall culminating the life of every man. I Corinthians 15:54 says, *"Death is swallowed up in victory."* There will be no more cause for sorrow, as tears will be taken from all faces. This is the future of Planet Earth.

The whole *world* will experience a healing:

> *"Moreover the light of the moon shall be as the light of the sun, and the light of the sun shall be sevenfold, as the light of seven days"* (Isa. 30:26).

There's something about light that is healing. Modern science has found that the ultraviolet component of even ordinary light has healing power. This passage of Scripture doesn't mention *heat,* it mentions *light.* And it talks about the healing of a wound in this same verse.

The entire world will be healed. The world is today groaning under nearly six thousand years of apostasy. But, thank God, all the terror that sin has caused, the painful wounds that have resulted, the very hearts and lives of the masses — and even the very earth itself — they're all going to be healed.

And now, listen to this:

> *"And the inhabitant shall not say, I am sick: the people that dwell therein shall be forgiven their iniquity"* (Isa. 33:24).

Thank God, no more sickness, no more of the terrible diseases afflicting mankind today. No one will have to say, "I am sick," for sickness will be utterly removed.

Sickness is another result of Adam's fall. Sickness is the seed of Satan. But it's over now — at last it's been done away with. Close down your local hospital and close down the companies producing medicines. Everyone is going to live in health. The inhabitants shall no longer say, "I am sick."

*"Then the eyes of the blind shall be opened,
and the ears of the deaf shall be unstopped.*

*"Then shall the lame man leap as an hart,
and the tongue of the dumb sing: for in the
wilderness shall waters break out, and streams
in the desert"* (Isa. 35:5, 6).

I have to shout *hallelujah* as I read this because the
world is *not* going to be destroyed in a sudden onslaught
of bloodletting and catastrophe as today's doom-criers
predict. *Glorious* days lie ahead for those who serve and
live for the Lord Jesus Christ.

The time is to be called the "Thousand-Year Reign of
Christ." It will be a reign of infinite prosperity, peace,
health, glory, and power. And the only way to be included is
to have your sins forgiven now and serve Him — the King
of kings and Lord of lords. Great things hath He prepared
for those who love Him.

SATAN LOOSED FOR A LITTLE SEASON

*"And I saw an angel come down from
heaven, having the key of the bottomless pit and
a great chain in his hand.*

*"And he laid hold on the dragon, that old
serpent, which is the Devil, and Satan, and
bound him a thousand years,*

*"And cast him into the bottomless pit, and
shut him up, and set a seal upon him, that he
should deceive the nations no more, till the thousand years should be fulfilled: and after that he
must be loosed a little season.*

*"And when the thousand years are expired,
Satan shall be loosed out of his prison,*

"And shall go out to deceive the nations

*which are in the four quarters of the earth, Gog
and Magog, to gather them together to battle:
the number of whom is as the sand of the sea.*

*"And they went up on the breadth of the
earth, and compassed the camp of the saints
about, and the beloved city: and fire came down
from God out of heaven, and devoured them"*
(Rev. 20:1-3, 7-9).

This is Satan's last gasp. He will be allowed (through
God's sufferance) out of the bottomless pit at the end of the
"Thousand-Year Reign" of Christ. At this time he will
gather together a company from the face of the earth that
has *served* God, but at the same time chose not to *live* for
Him. These were forced to *obey* the laws but in their hearts
did not desire righteousness. They will be delighted by
Satan's influence when he once again battles the Lord Jesus
Christ at the city of Jerusalem.

How long will this battle last? The Bible does not say.
From the description, however, it would seem to be of very
short duration. This won't really be a battle in the sense one
would ordinarily picture a battle. Satan will try to mount a
siege — but Scripture describes fire coming down from
heaven and devouring them.

It also says in Revelation 20:10 that the devil will then
be cast into the lake of fire and brimstone, and that he shall
be tormented day and night forever.

Finally the world sees the end of Satan. He will never
again be allowed to torment the world.

THE GREAT WHITE THRONE JUDGMENT

*"And I saw a great white throne, and him that
sat on it, from whose face the earth and the heaven
fled away; and there was found no place for them.*

> *"And I saw the dead, small and great, stand before God; and the books were opened: and another book was opened, which is the book of life: and the dead were judged out of those things which were written in the books, according to their works.*
>
> *"And the sea gave up the dead which were in it; and death and hell delivered up the dead which were in them: and they were judged every man according to their works.*
>
> *"And death and hell were cast into the lake of fire. This is the second death"* (Rev. 20:11-14)

This is called the second resurrection of damnation, or the Great White Throne Judgment. The location for this judgment would seem to be in heaven. God and His Son, Jesus Christ, will judge the unsaved appearing before the Great White Throne. Individuals who have lived without God will stand there for judgment, according to the lives they have lived. Not a single one will be pardoned — all will be thrown into the lake of fire.

Of course, the question must be asked: "Why bother having this judgment if none will be spared?" The Great White Throne Judgment will take place simply because of the immaculate justice of God. God is eternally and everlastingly just. No one will be able to complain or make excuses. The books will be thrown open and everyone will be able to see exactly what he has done and the opportunities he has missed. No one will be able to accuse God of being unfair or unjust. This is the reason for the Great White Throne Judgment.

Some people are mistaken in the belief that there will be Christians at the Great White Throne Judgment. They feel that Christians will also come for judgment, and that some will be lost and some saved. This is completely untrue. No Christian will be judged, as our (Christians') sins have already been blotted out by the precious blood of the Lord Jesus Christ. Only the *unsaved* will be at the Great White Throne Judgment. So, as far as the Great White Throne Judgment is concerned, not one single child of God will be there. It is only for those whose names are not found written in the Lamb's Book of Life.

THE NEW HEAVEN AND THE NEW EARTH

> *"And I saw a new heaven and a new earth: for the first heaven and the first earth were passed away; and there was no more sea.*
>
> *"And I John saw the holy city, new Jerusalem, coming down from God out of heaven, prepared as a bride adorned for her husband.*
>
> *"And I heard a great voice out of heaven saying, Behold, the tabernacle of God is with men, and he will dwell with them, and they shall be his people, and God himself shall be with them, and be their God.*
>
> *"And God shall wipe away all tears from their eyes; and there shall be no more death, neither sorrow, nor crying, neither shall there be any more pain: for the former things are passed away.*
>
> *"And he that sat upon the throne said, Behold, I make all things new. And he said unto me, Write: for these words are true and faithful"*
> (Rev. 21:1-5)

At the end of the millennial reign, after Satan's last uprising and after the Great White Throne Judgment, God will *"create a new heaven and a new earth."* This doesn't mean He is going to completely do away with the present ones. Rather, it will be a renovation that will occur. The Greek word is *parerchomai*. This means "to pass from one condition to another." It does not mean total annihilation; it means precisely what it says: a change in condition.

There will be dramatic changes. For example, there will be no more great oceans such as the Atlantic and the Pacific. But the most dramatic change of all will be that there will never again be the opportunity for rebellion against God. Disobedience and all evil will totally and eternally be banished from Planet Earth.

And there is still one more dramatic occurrence to stun men's minds. The marvelous New Jerusalem is going to come down from heaven, transferring God the Father's throne from heaven to earth. New Jerusalem will be some fifteen hundred miles square. Picture that: a *city* half the size of the United States.

God will change His headquarters from heaven to New Jerusalem on earth and He will rule and reign in total righteousness and love, among men, forever and forever.

THIS IS THE FUTURE OF PLANET EARTH.

So, knowing what the Bible predicts as the outcome for these troubled days, we have no cause to fear. It's a *glorious* future, a future so startling in concept that it beggars description.

Only God could bring about such a stunning transformation, and this is exactly what is going to happen. Satan has nearly run his course; the day of worldly madness is about to come to an end. The time is soon coming when the earth shall be covered by the knowledge of the Lord, as the waters cover the sea.

THE MOST IMPORTANT QUESTION

But the most important question of all is, "Will *you* be ready for it?" And it is a question that each person must answer for himself.

The only way you can make your calling and election sure is by accepting Jesus Christ as your personal Saviour. There is no other way. If you do not accept Jesus as Lord and Master of *your* life, you will have chosen perdition and everlasting judgment. If you *do* accept Him:

> *"Eye hath not seen, nor ear heard, neither have entered into the heart of man, the things which God hath prepared for them that love him"* (I Cor. 2:9).

The decision is yours. The future is unlimited — so bountiful that human words are incapable of describing it. But there *is* a requirement for admission, and that is acceptance of Jesus Christ and His saving blood into your heart and life.

And the *time* for that decision? *Today* is the acceptable day of the Lord.